To Louie

D1622665

LINCOLN SPEAKS
TO LEADERS

LMJ

LINCOLN SPEAKS
TO LEADERS

20 Powerful Lessons for Today's Leaders from America's 16th President

By GENE GRIESSMAN *and* PAT WILLIAMS
with PEGGY MATTHEWS ROSE

ELEVATE®
A PART OF ADVANTAGE MEDIA GROUP

Published by Elevate, Charleston, South Carolina.
Member of Advantage Media Group.

ELEVATE is a registered trademark and the Elevate colophon is a trademark of Advantage Media Group, Inc.

Printed in the United States of America.

ISBN: 978-1-60194-028-5

Most Advantage Media Group titles are available at special quantity discounts for bulk purchases for sales promotions, premiums, fundraising, and educational use. Special versions or book excerpts can also be created to fit specific needs.

For more information, please write: Special Markets, Advantage Media Group, P.O. Box 272, Charleston, SC 29402 or call 1.866.775.1696.

Visit us online at **advantagefamily**.com

Library of Congress Cataloging-in-Publication Data
Griessman, Gene.
Lincoln speaks to leaders : 20 powerful lessons for today's leaders from America's 16th president / by Gene Griessman and Pat Williams with Peggy Matthews Rose.
    p. cm.
 ISBN 978-1-60194-028-5
1. Lincoln, Abraham, 1809-1865—Political and social views. 2. Lincoln, Abraham, 1809-1865—Philosophy. 3. Political leadership—United States. 4. Leadership—United States. 5. Conduct of life. I. Williams, Pat, 1940- II. Rose, Peggy Matthews. III. Title.
 E457.2.G85 2009
 973.7092--dc22
                         2008048680

I dedicate this book to Coach John Wooden, legendary UCLA basketball coach and another great American hero. His love for Abraham Lincoln helped inspire my own.

—Pat Williams

I dedicate this book to Sharon Griessman— beloved daughter, astute business partner, unselfish friend.

—Gene Griessman, Ph.D.

A unique and fascinating examination of how the life and lessons of our greatest president are more relevant than ever for leaders of our own troubled time. Lincoln Speaks to Leaders *is inspiring, engrossing, and a sure-fire best-seller.*

—STEPHEN B. OATES, Author of *With Malice Toward None: The Life Of Abraham Lincoln and Lincoln: The Man Behind The Myths*

What a novel concept! A top Lincoln impersonator teaches us valuable leadership principles, and a top sports executive offers his advice on applying them in our daily activities. This book will have a major impact for a long time.

—DAVID PIETRUSZA, Author of 1960—LBJ vs. JFK vs. Nixon

Two hundred years after his birth, Abraham Lincoln still fascinates and inspires us. In Lincoln Speaks to Leaders, *Gene Griessman and Pat Williams show how Lincoln's example can point the way to more effective leadership in our own time. Drawing on history and personal experience, Griessman (as Abraham Lincoln) and Williams highlight the traits and habits that helped Lincoln meet the extraordinary challenges of his day. In the process, they remind us that those same traits – the resolve to succeed, a command of the language, and a willingness to learn from experience, to name a few – are necessary ingredients for success in any age. This important book is not just a lesson in self-improvement, it's a refreshing new way to learn from America's greatest leader.*

—MICHAEL W. KAUFFMAN, Author, *American Brutus: John Wilkes Booth and the Lincoln Conspiracies*

Pat Williams and Gene Griessman have put together a leadership book for the ages. It's amazing to hear Abraham Lincoln speak so clearly about issues that are relevant to all of us today.

—HOUSTON NUTT, Head Football Coach, University of Mississippi

'Mr. Lincoln' and Pat Williams have teamed up and written a classic. The leadership lessons in this book will elevate every leader to another level—including me!

—GARY KUBIAK, Head Coach, Houston Texans

This book is must reading for anyone in a leadership position. There is nothing more important than strong leadership in every organization and team. Who better to learn from than Abraham Lincoln, one of America's greatest presidents!

—JAY WRIGHT, Head Men's Basketball Coach, Villanova University

Abraham Lincoln's leadership ability still inspires us today. Gene Griessman and Pat Williams have done all of us a great service by writing this book. These lessons will be read, studied, and applied for years to come.

—BARRY ALVAREZ, Athletic Director, University of Wisconsin

You will never read a more interesting or practical book on leadership. Hearing Mr. Lincoln's voice in 2009 inspired me beyond words. Get ready for a life-changing reading experience.

—KIRK FERENTZ, Head Football Coach, University of Iowa

Clearly my appreciation for Abraham Lincoln's leadership principles has been enhanced through my friendship with Coach John Wooden. During my twelve years coaching basketball at UCLA Coach Wooden often referred to Lincoln as his favorite American and quoted him on a regular basis as a vehicle to teach others who were willing to listen. Now we can all improve our ability to lead through reading this excellent new book written by Pat Williams and Gene Griessman.

—STEVE LAVIN, Former UCLA basketball coach, Basketball analyst and broadcaster, ABC/ESPN

There are many challenges to being a successful leader. Lincoln Speaks to Leaders *explores the many facets of leadership in a unique way. Leaders of today and tomorrow will enjoy this book.*

—ROMEO CRENNEL, Head Coach, Cleveland Browns

This book positively vibrates with Pat Williams' deep commitment to the story of Abraham Lincoln, and to the powerful lessons in leadership and life that he and Gene Griessman have derived from Lincoln's example.

—GERALD J. PROKOPOWICZ, J.D., PH.D., History Department Chair, East Carolina University, Author, *Did Lincoln Own Slaves?*

Abraham Lincoln has always been a hero to me. Gene Griessman and my friend Pat Williams have brought him alive in a way I never could have imagined. After reading this fascinating material, you will be destined for great leadership success.

—JEREMY FOLEY, Athletics Director, University of Florida

I am now living and coaching at the University of Illinois, right in the middle of Lincoln country. After reading this new book about Lincoln's leadership style, I am more inspired than ever to lead like Mr. Lincoln. You will be, too; I promise.

—RON ZOOK, Head Football Coach, University of Illinois

As a student of history, there are so many applications from our American heritage that apply to leaders today. Gene Griessman and Pat Williams have captured the essence of Abraham Lincoln's leadership skills in this highly readable and enjoyable book. Best of all, these two talented writers teach us how to apply Lincoln's leadership lessons. All of us are better for it.

—SKIP HOLTZ, Head Football Coach, East Carolina University

Few figures in American history have faced as many obstacles and as much opposition as Abraham Lincoln—and even fewer have matched his executive abilities. Lincoln Speaks to Leaders *skillfully equips today's reader with the legacy of leadership that made Lincoln great.*

—ROD GRAGG, Author, *The Civil War Quiz & Fact Book*

Abraham Lincoln was, undoubtedly, one of our great leaders. It's no surprise that taking important lessons from this great leader will be very rewarding as you try to improve every area of your life.

—BRIAN FRANCE, Chairman and CEO, NASCAR

This book on Abraham Lincoln's leadership style is loaded with great material. The wisdom and insights in this book presented by Gene Griessman and Pat Williams are incredible. I will be recommending this book to coaches and players.

—JACK DEL RIO, Head Coach, Jacksonville Jaguars

CONTENTS

INTRODUCTION

All my life, I've been fascinated by Abraham Lincoln—as a leader, as a president, and as a man whose life was a powerful influence, both in his own time and beyond. I've read many books about him—biographies, history books, and books that contain his wisdom. So you can imagine how I felt one morning in October of 2007 when I was speaking at the Blue Ridge Conference on Leadership just outside of Asheville, North Carolina. I sat in an audience of fellow business leaders and heard Lincoln's stirring words and principles zinging their way to my heart—straight from the mouth of Abraham Lincoln himself!

Or so it most certainly seemed.

The man I heard was actually Gene Griessman, a renowned Lincoln scholar, leadership expert, and an actor skilled in presenting his one-man Lincoln show. His ability to both look and sound like the Great Emancipator himself was completely convincing, and the audience was captivated. As it happened, I was the afternoon keynote speaker at that conference—but, wow, was Dr. Griessman's Lincoln a tough act to follow. I could not let the opportunity it presented pass me by. So I met with Dr. Griessman to propose this book you now hold in your hands. I'm so grateful he agreed. I believe the lessons we present here have the power to change your life dramatically, whether or not you're currently in a leadership position. By the way, if you are you will find your life and leadership style significantly enhanced by what you read, learn, and apply from this book.

February 12, 2009 marks the 200th birthday of Abraham Lincoln, America's sixteenth president and a principle architect of the Republican Party. He led the country through its time of greatest division, after making clear to those who pressed for civil war that the consequences were in *their* hands and not his. For him the call was to stand for what was right and work to hold the Union together. "You have no oath registered in Heaven to destroy the government," he said, "while I shall have the most solemn one to preserve, protect, and defend it."

What a fitting time to inspire America's current and future leaders with lessons from Lincoln's own lips. The chapters in this book are based on selected principles from Dr. Griessman's unique presentation, and are followed by summaries in which I distill leadership lessons for contemporary readers.

In many ways, this book was inspired by the first book to bring Lincoln's leadership skills to a mass audience and the book that single-handedly created the leadership section now found in contemporary book stores—*Lincoln on Leadership: Executive Strategies for Tough Times* (Warner Books 1992), by Donald T. Phillips. That little gem revolutionized the leadership book genre by holding up the principles we'd all been learning in the light of a man who modeled straight-talking, right-thinking, servant leadership as few have ever done. We owe a debt to Phillips' pioneering work, and I personally am grateful to him for helping me see this great man as not just a historical figure, but as a role model for my own leadership style.

And now, Gene Griessman and I are pleased to offer you stories and lessons inspired by Lincoln himself, as if the Great Emancipator and I sat side-by-side to write them. It's one thing to read *about* a leader like Lincoln—but in this book you will actually hear Lincoln's wisdom, *from* Lincoln. And in the bargain, you'll gain insight for your own leadership role.

I cannot think of a better occasion for a book like this than the 200th birthday of this great man, at a time when our nation and its leaders need to resolve afresh that, in Lincoln's own words, "these dead shall not have died in vain—that this nation, under God, shall have a new birth of freedom—and that government of the people, by the people, for the people, shall not perish from the earth."

—*Pat Williams, Orlando, Florida*

FEBRUARY 2009

CHAPTER 1:

HISTORY LESSONS TO PROFIT BY

··

Lincoln's Logs, by Gene Griessman

My name is Lincoln—Abraham Lincoln. And I've been dead for well over a century.

I was born in Kentucky in 1809, moved with my family to Indiana in 1816, and to Illinois in 1830. I tried my hand at several occupations, with limited or no success, and eventually became a lawyer, a politician, and finally the sixteenth President of the United States. I led the nation through the wrenching division of the Civil War, issued the Emancipation Proclamation, and was assassinated on Good Friday of 1865 by John Wilkes Booth, while attending a play at Ford's Theatre.

I was not known for my good looks. A woman once came up to me and said, "You're the ugliest man I've ever seen in my life!" I told her, "I can't help it." "Be that as it may," she said, "you *could* stay home!"

But I am observant, and one thing I have observed is that history sometimes seems to repeat itself. For example, there are a number of parallels between my life and the life of John F. Kennedy:

- I was elected president in 1860; Kennedy was elected president in 1960.

- My first office, U.S. House of Representatives, 1847; Mr. Kennedy's first office—U.S. House of Representatives, 1947.

- My name was put forward unsuccessfully for the Vice Presidency in 1856. Mr. Kennedy's name was put forward unsuccessfully for the Vice Presidency in 1956.

- I lost one son in the White House—little Willie. Mr. Kennedy lost one son in the White House—Patrick.

- I had no executive experience prior to becoming President; neither did Mr. Kennedy.

- I loved poetry; so did Mr. Kennedy.

- I was assassinated on Friday, while seated beside my wife. Mr. Kennedy was assassinated on Friday, while seated beside his wife.

- There are seven letters in the name Kennedy; there are seven letters in the name Lincoln.

- There are fifteen letters in the name John Wilkes Booth; there are fifteen letters in the name Lee Harvey Oswald. John Wilkes Booth kept a diary; Lee Harvey Oswald kept a diary. Both men were shot before they could be brought to trial.

- The same carriage used to transport my body to its final resting place was used for the same purpose for Mr. Kennedy's body.

- Mr. Kennedy's personal secretary from the day he was elected to the day he was assassinated was named—Lincoln—Evelyn Lincoln.

- And Mr. Kennedy's speech writer, Ted Sorenson, was born in Lincoln, Nebraska.

- My wife, Mary, spoke French; Jackie Kennedy spoke French. My wife loved fashionable, expensive clothes; Jackie Kennedy loved fashionable, expensive clothes. Mary redecorated the White House; Jackie Kennedy redecorated the White House.

- President Kennedy was succeeded in office by his Vice President, a Democrat, a man from the South named Johnson—Lyndon Johnson, who was born in 1908. I was succeeded by my Vice President—a Democrat from the South named Johnson— Andrew Johnson, born in 1808.

- And one final, silly little irony—Mr. Kennedy was riding in a Lincoln when he was shot.

That last one puts the whole thing in perspective, doesn't it?

The reason I mention these similarities is to get your attention, and to demonstrate that there is repetition in history. Some of the repetition is random, nothing more than coincidences.

But some of the repetition in history is not coincidental—it is causal. We live in a cause-and-effect universe. The same cause produces the same effect over and over again.

At least one source notes that Abraham Lincoln's firstborn son Robert, the only Lincoln child to reach adulthood, was saved from a potentially deadly accident by John Wilkes Booth's brother. It is recorded that Edwin Booth, a staunch Unionist well known to the younger Lincoln, rescued Robert Todd Lincoln in 1863 or 1864. Robert Lincoln later wrote an account of the incident for *The Century* magazine in 1909.

History is a Story

I've always been fascinated by history. If you don't like history, perhaps it's because you had a history teacher who taught you it was about memorizing dates, battles, and names of famous people. But history is much *more* than that.

It's possible you've come to believe that history is a book. History may be written *in* books, but history is more than a book.

History is a story—a story about people like you and me making choices or not making choices, and the results.

History is what happened 500 years ago. History is what happened five years ago. History is what happened…five *minutes* ago.

The world today seems different from the world I left in April of 1865. Yet in many ways, not that much has changed. Today's plays have the same plots as those performed in the 1800s. Only the names have been changed. The human condition remains the same.

When I read today's newspapers, the crime, the politics and the scandals, sound remarkably like those from the newspapers of the 1800s. Individuals—and nations—still pursue their own interests. People still love and hate, are generous and petty, trusting and suspicious, tolerant and judgmental, honest and crooked, kind and vicious.

Rulers still send their young people off to war. Both sides still believe that they fight for a good cause—for God and country and lofty principles—just as they always have.

All believe that God is with them, and both sides invoke God's aid against the other. The prayers of both cannot be answered.

I hope the Lord is on our side. I am not at all concerned about that, for I know that the Lord is always on the side of the right. But it is my constant anxiety and prayer that I and this nation should be on the Lord's side.

— A. LINCOLN,
TO A GROUP OF MINISTERS VISITING THE WHITE HOUSE

History's story is often a sad one, but not always. History tells us people can be deceived, but not all the people all the time. For me, that's a hopeful lesson from history.

History can tell us what to look for if we're brave enough to open our eyes and ears. An enormous amount of historical information has been collected about successful leaders and unsuccessful ones. It almost begs us to learn from it. In business schools, I'm told students read what they call "case studies." If you think about it, a case study is really a little piece of history—a detailed account of choices that were made or not made, and the results.

I love science and technology. In fact, I take some pride in the fact that I still am the only President who holds a patent. In case you're interested, it was for a floatation device that could be used to lift ships off shoals and sandbars. I thought of the need for it when I was working as a bargeman on the Ohio and Mississippi Rivers.

You use history if you're an inventor. If you're clever, you begin your project by finding out what has already been done with the problem, and what have been the results.

Effective leaders can make use of history. Leadership is science and art. Good leaders use principles that have been discovered and used with good results in the past. One of my successors, President Harry Truman, put it this way, "The only new thing in the world is the history you don't know."

Living Lincoln: History's Lessons
By Pat Williams

The lessons of history are there for us to draw from, no question. When we ignore them, we do so to our own disadvantage and detriment. I can't truthfully answer Lincoln's question about whether or not history repeats itself as specifically as the incidences he cites regarding himself and John F. Kennedy, though it's interesting to note that the officially recorded ending dates for Civil War and the Civil Rights Movement are exactly 100 years apart—in 1865 and 1965 respectively. Of course, it took much longer for both conflicts to end in the minds of many people, but the point is—historical patterns do repeat. The evidence is abundant.

For instance, we can pretty much count on real estate going through up-and-down cycles every seven to ten years, not unlike the seven fat years followed by the seven lean years in the familiar story of Joseph, recorded in the biblical book of Genesis. Similarly, the economy will do well for a time and will be rocky for a few years—regardless of what president or party is in office. History also records the cyclical rise and fall of kingdoms and government systems.

The reason for this, as Lincoln pointed out, is that human nature hasn't really changed much over the years. We can know that, given the same set of circumstances, social and cultural behavior is likely to follow the same patterns in the future as it has for ages past. What *can* change, if we so choose, is our personal behavior, our personal leadership style. Together, we *can* make a difference—one that ends in a better tomorrow. Here's how:

Imagine Abraham Lincoln at the head of your personal cavalry, or as your teacher hammering a lesson home. With a leader like Lincoln as your guide, you're on the right road. Mark its path well, so you'll recognize it the next time you pass this way.

So what does this matter to you? If you and I are going to be men and women of positive, lasting influence, we've got to study history. It helps us recognize the patterns, passions, and practices that lead to success, and it shows us how to avoid the traps that doom us to failure. In short, studying history helps us understand precedents in human behavior, thereby helping us make wiser choices for the future.

The more you understand about what's worked and what's gone wrong up to now, the better prepared you'll be to lead your team into the end zone—no matter what giant defensive linemen may block your path.

Lincoln Lessons for Today

Wisdom to Apply Right Now

1. **Challenge yourself to read** at least one history book or biography a month.

2. **Study the chronicles**—the history, if you will—of your country, your state, your community, or your company. Understanding the past illuminates the future.

3. **Learn to identify the key players**, the men and women who left the legacy you have inherited. What would they have you do with that trust?

4. **Look for "case studies" when you read.** Ask these questions about each one: what were problems that the leaders faced; what did they want to get or what did they hope to achieve; what alternative tactics or strategies did they consider; what did they actually do or not do; what were the results; and why.

CHAPTER 2:

WHAT TO DO WHEN RELATIONSHIPS GO BAD

....

Lincoln's Logs, by Gene Griessman

Let me tell you about my wife Mary—Mary Todd Lincoln.

Mary came from the wealthy, aristocratic Todd family. Mind you, that's Todd, with two D's. God needed only one D for his name, but the Todd family needed two.

Mary grew up in an imposing two-story brick mansion with English bone china, and French crystal, and Belgian linens. She studied the classics, and went to finishing school. She could read and speak French. Mary was comfortable with the rich and the mighty.

From her childhood, Mary told people that one day she would be the first lady—the wife of the President. She dreamed of living in the White House, and told people so.

When I was courting Mary, she was also being courted by Stephen Douglas. If you know American history, you know the name Stephen Douglas. Stephen Douglas had already become well known as a politician by the time I started courting Mary.

Somebody asked Mary which one of us she would marry, and she replied, "The one that has the best chance of becoming President."

How's that for true love!

I subsequently ran against Stephen Douglas for the U.S. Senate, and lost. I ran against Stephen Douglas for President, and won.

I wonder how she recognized my presidential talents so early?

The truth is, anybody who married Mary Todd would have become President. She would have nagged 'em to death if they hadn't.

It seemed to him manifest destiny. "I will get there," he would say, seemingly in the fullest confidence of realizing his prediction.

— WARD HILL LAMON,
LINCOLN'S LAWYER, FRIEND, AND CONFIDANT ON
LINCOLN'S DRIVE TO BECOME PRESIDENT

Actually I did what several Presidents have done. I married up. George Washington married up. John Adams married up. So did Harry Truman, and Lyndon Johnson, and Ronald Reagan.

In Mary's case, the fact that she had been to finishing school, and could move in middle-class and upper-class circles, gave her knowledge and social skills that I did not possess. I started at the bottom rung of the ladder. She tried to give me a bit of polish, tried to teach me how to comport myself in polite circles—with limited success—and it helped.

Many of my friends didn't like Mary. They thought she was too high-strung, too opinionated, too haughty.

But I loved her. Not like my first love, Ann Rutledge. Ann died when we were young—of a fever, when we both lived in the village of New Salem, Illinois. She was only twenty-two, with beautiful blue eyes, long, flowing chestnut-colored hair, a kind, gentle spirit.

When they lowered Ann's casket into the grave, my heart was inside. For the longest time I could not bear to think of her body lying out there in the cold and the rain.

But I learned to love Mary. She truly cared about me, and tried to make me a better man, and for that I was grateful.

That doesn't mean that we always got along very well. We didn't.

Once she verbally abused a repairman so fiercely that he demanded an apology from me. I told him. "What? Can't you put up with fifteen minutes of what I've been putting up with for fifteen years?" He ended up expressing sympathy to me.

That reminds me of a story, about an old man who went in for a physical examination. When it was done, the doctor told him that he was in excellent health for a man his age. "Is there a secret?"

"Yep…When my wife and I got married, we made a promise to one another that if we ever lost our temper at the same time, I'd take a long walk…I owe my excellent health to my many years of outdoor life." Like that old man, I spent a lot of time outside the house.

I suppose if my home life had been more pleasant, I would have wanted to stay home more, and I would not have become what people in the 1800s called "a public man."

If I had married Ann Rutledge, I would probably have been a happier man, but I certainly would never have become President of the United States.

Living Lincoln:
When Relationships Go Bad
By Pat Williams

Lincoln's life did not turn out as he'd expected it would when he was young. Let me ask you this: whose does?

But in time he discovered that it turned out just as it should have—with the possible exception of his premature death.

I say "possible" because I believe that for the most part, things happen when they're supposed to. I also believe people come into our lives because they are supposed to. Whether good or bad, rocky or smooth, relationships are designed to teach us how to be better people. Let me share a story that might illustrate what I mean.

In 1973, I began to sense my career with the Chicago Bulls was coming to an end. I'd been in the front office with the team since 1969 and it had been a definite rollercoaster ride. But this year, the Bulls' multimillionaire owner, Arthur Wirtz, decided to become more "hands on" in his relationship with the team. That was, of course, his right, but in my mind his style was intrusive and intimidating. To put it bluntly, we did not see eye-to-eye.

Now, of course, a job is not the same as a marriage—which is the kind of partnership Lincoln is talking about here—but the principle is the same: even a bad professional alliance can have its benefits. The key is that you continually seek wisdom for your direction, avoid compromising your present position, and take advantage of networking opportunities. Having been in both positions—a bad job and a bad marriage—I believe I can say those techniques work in both situations. But I digress.

As my job with the Bulls became more and more frustrating, several of my colleagues in other parts of the sports world heard I might be willing to make a move—that, by the way, is the magic of networking. Before long, I found myself with very attractive offers from both the Baltimore Orioles and the Atlanta Hawks, so my days of Chicago chagrin were almost over. I ended up going with the Hawks in a move that eventually led me to my longest and best run before helping to found the Orlando Magic—twelve years as general manager of the Philadelphia 76ers. It would have been easy to remain a bitter Bull, but I wouldn't trade my Magic life for anything.

So I managed to stay in the NBA and my career continued to climb, in spite of that rocky time at the end of my Chicago experience. But I learned a valuable lesson from my less-than-glorious parting. By the time I'd left the Bulls, I'd been with the team four years and had done more than my share to revive an organization that had been dying before I showed up. Yet for all that, on my last day, all I got from the Bulls' owner Arthur Wirtz, whose micro-managing style had contributed to so much of my grief, was his backside after I'd signed the document terminating our relationship.

Why lead that way when you have a choice? Because of his cold demeanor, I will always have a less than warm fuzzy feeling when I think about that man. Not exactly the kind of legacy I want to leave. How about you? Thanks to Arthur Wirtz, I learned that as much as it's up to me, I never want to leave that kind of bad taste in anyone's mouth.

That Wirtz story reminds me of the time Bear Bryant was coaching football at the University of Kentucky, toiling away in the shadow of Adolph Rupp, the great basketball coach. So enamored were the Kentucky fans of their basketball team that no matter what Bryant did, he couldn't compete with Rupp. After one particularly good season, Rupp was awarded with a Cadillac, while Bryant received a cigarette lighter. That was it for Bryant. He left Kentucky for Texas A&M, and from there to Alabama. The rest is history.

So the lesson here is that even bad relationships can lead you in directions that are ultimately in your best interest, and they can benefit others in either a direct or roundabout way. It's important also to note that in every bad relationship there is a potential for reconciliation. In fact, I recommend doing what you can to build a bridge of friendship—but we'll talk more about that in Chapter 13.

Lincoln Lessons for Today

Wisdom to Apply Right Now

1. **Take another look at relationships in your life** that might seem on the surface to be disastrous. Recognize that being associated with difficult people is part of the human experience. Some relationships may start out beautifully and turn sour—a marriage or a business partnership. Some relationships may prove difficult from the beginning—a boss or commanding officer whose leadership skills are poor. Still others—and these are more rare—begin terribly and end up filled with respect, admiration, and sometimes, even love.

2. **Recognize that everyone in your life is there for a reason**—to help shape you into a better leader and human being. Lincoln frequently quoted the couplet: "There's *a divinity that shapes our ends*, Rough-hew them as we will."

3. **Look for ways to benefit from the bad** times and the bad experiences, as Lincoln did on those long walks.

4. **See if there isn't some way to learn** to love the unique qualities built inside even the most difficult people you know.

5. **See if there isn't some benefit** you can derive from an unpleasant association, something you can learn, some contact you can make, some choice you can avoid making a second time—something that puts that relationship into the win column in your life.

6. **Evaluate every relationship in terms of whether it makes you want to be a better person.** Ask yourself, *Does this person (or group) bring out the best or the worst in me?* Minimize your contacts with individuals or groups that push you to do bad things, and seriously consider terminating the relationship if things don't change.

7. **Evaluate every relationship in terms of whether or not it makes you feel good about yourself.** Look for people who celebrate you, not just tolerate you. Lincoln did that with Ward Lamon, a long-time friend who was unlike Lincoln in many ways, but helped Lincoln through difficult times by his unqualified loyalty and respect.

8. **Submit your relationships to cost-benefit analysis.** Relationships that bring you little or nothing should be terminated. However, some that are scratchy and difficult may be worth maintaining because of the positives that you derive from them.

CHAPTER 3:

THE BENEFITS OF SLOW THINKING

....

Lincoln's Logs, by Gene Griessman

I was always a slow thinker. In fact, Billy Herndon, my long-time law partner, said I even walked like I needed oiling. He said if I tried to think too fast, the machinery jammed.

If you're a slow thinker, there's no reason to be embarrassed about it. There are advantages. You make fewer mistakes. Making decisions too quickly can be a great folly. Wisdom is more important than brilliance.

I was a slow thinker, but I was a deliberate, methodical thinker.

To use an analogy from surveying (I was a surveyor for a while), I was never happy with an idea until I had bounded it north, and bounded it south, and bounded it east, and bounded it west. Or to use an analogy from farming, I wanted to dig up an idea and examine it by the roots.

Nothing valuable can be lost by taking time. If there be any object to hurry any of you, in hot haste, to a step which you would never take deliberately, that object will be frustrated by taking time; but no good object can be frustrated by it.

– A. LINCOLN,
FIRST INAUGURAL ADDRESS

When I was a mere child, I used to get irritated when anybody talked to me in a way that I could not understand. I'd sometimes lie in my bed at night and turn the words over and over in my mind, until I thought I understood them, and then I would put the idea in language plain enough, as I thought, for any boy I knew to comprehend.

My son Willie thought in the same manner that I did. People said Willie was like me in many ways, and the way we processed ideas was one of them. Once in the White House, I put a problem to Willie. He was silent for quite a while. Then he smiled and gave me his answer. I told a guest who was present: I know every step of the process by which that boy arrived at his solution.

It is by just such slow methods that I attain results.

How the Union Benefitted from Lincoln's Slow Thinking

In a letter to General Tecumseh Sherman following his dramatic March to the Sea, as the 1864 Savannah Campaign has come to be known, Lincoln acknowledged his apprehension regarding that event, which proceeded unhindered as a result of Lincoln's slow thinking ways.

"My dear General Sherman. Many, many thanks for your Christmas gift—the capture of Savannah. When you were about leaving Atlanta for the Atlantic coast, I was anxious, if not fearful; but feeling that you were the better judge, and remember that 'nothing risked, nothing gained,' I did not interfere. Now the undertaking being a success, the honor is all yours; for I believe none of us went farther than to acquiesce...."

Possibility Thinking

I am a possibility thinker.

Growing up on the frontier, early on I learned that there were few ready-made solutions. If you needed clothes, you had to make them. If you wanted to eat, you found wild fruit, hunted game, or cultivated crops. If you needed a boat, you built it. If you weren't resourceful, nature's response could be unforgiving, brutal, final.

When I was in my early twenties, two relatives and I entered into an agreement with a local businessman to take a boat full of cargo down the Sangamon River to the Illinois River and on to the Mississippi River and eventually New Orleans. After constructing the boat, we loaded it with corn, barrels of pork, and some "hawgs," and embarked on our adventure.

Unfortunately, the Sangamon River was full of obstacles, and not long after launching our boat we snagged on a low milldam. There we were with the front end of the boat sticking out over the dam, and the back end filling up with water. The terrified, squealing hogs added to the drama. All seemed lost—boat and cargo. A crowd gathered on the river-bank to watch. Somehow we managed to get all our cargo off the boat and on to the shore—all except the heavy barrels of pork.

I had an idea. Why not roll the barrels to the front of the boat, so that all the water could slosh to the front of the boat—which is what we did. I then drilled a hole in the bottom of the front of the boat, which allowed the water to drain out. The boat, because it was lighter, slid right over the dam. I then plugged up the hole, we reloaded the cargo, and were soon on our way—to the cheers of the large crowd that had assembled.

That experience, and others like it, increased my self-confidence. I came to believe that I could do anything that any other person could do. I believed in myself, in my capacities, and my powers.

Years later, when I was serving in Congress, I supported a bill to construct bridges, roads, and canals, and in my remarks quoted a Roman writer by the name of Terence, who said: "Attempt the end, and never stand to doubt. Nothing so hard, but search will find it out." My motto: "Determine that the thing can and shall be done, and we shall find the way."

Look at things not as they are, but as they can be. Visualization adds value to everything. A big thinker always visualizes what can be done in the future. He isn't stuck with the present.[1]

D A V I D   J .   S C H W A R T Z ,   P H . D .

Living Lincoln: Leaders are Thinkers!
By Pat Williams

In our fast-paced world where our thoughts are manipulated daily by leaders, peers, and the media, what great advice this is! We might not all be born "slow thinkers" like Lincoln, but we can learn to slow down and think things though more clearly. Consider the advantages to the outcome of our choices if we learn to consider all the facts before we take the leap. Lincoln and I challenge you to slow down and discover that wisdom is more important than brilliance.

---

1   *The Magic of Thinking Big*, by David J. Schwartz. New York: Fireside, Simon & Schuster, 1959. First FIRESIDE EDITION, 1987, p. 71.

In 1965 I was named general manager of the Spartanburg Phillies farm club team. Two local businessmen—G. Leo Hughes and R.E. Little-john—owned the Spartanburg team. And in my four years working with them I was introduced to fast thinking and slow thinking. Mr. Hughes was a fast-thinker—very impulsive. When something would happen he would react immediately, often publicly. Sometimes he might even "fast think" to the newspaper. I remember one time he sounded off to the sports editor Ed McGrath. The opening sentence of McGrath's column went, "Gosh golly gee, Leo! You really *are* in an uproar." G. Leo Hughes was a fast thinker.

Mr. Littlejohn, on the other hand, was a slow thinker—always calm, always under control, rarely voiced an opinion immediately. I loved to watch him in meetings—a board meeting, a bank meeting, a baseball gathering—he would sit, he would listen, absorb, not say anything. He was always the last to speak. He wanted to get every bit of input channeled into his mind so he could mull it over, analyze it, evaluate it. Everybody in the room knew he'd be last to speak. They also knew what he was going to say would make great sense and probably would be the way to go. Inevitably that's what happened. Mr. Littlejohn was a slow thinker.

Donnie Walsh is the president of the New York Knicks, after spending many years in the same position with the Indiana Pacers. Donnie is known in the NBA as a slow thinker. He is very deliberate and patient before deciding what to do. Once his mind is made up, he moves forward very aggressively. I see that same quality in my son Bobby, who is farm director for the Washington Nationals. He's a young man, but thinks things through in a very careful and thorough manner before making his decisions.

It's important not to dilly-dally around when a decision *must* be made *now*, that is for sure. But when time is on your side, you can only benefit from slow thinking. Let the facts simmer awhile before you spout off. Be the kind of leader who, like Mr. R.E. Littlejohn, makes the call everyone agrees makes great sense and is usually the way to go.

Lincoln Lessons for Today

Wisdom to Apply Right Now

1. **Slow down!** A friend of mine recently noted, on listening to someone's vast life experience outlined, "How could he have time for all that? I spend almost every waking moment working!" Friend, don't let that be you—working much and accomplishing little. Whatever you're doing—slow down!

2. **Take time to decide.** Beware of decisions made in haste—even if they seem right at the moment. Learn to be a slow, methodical thinker, to "never be happy with an idea until" you have it completely surrounded—"bounded it north, and bounded it south, and bounded it east, and bounded it west." Like Lincoln, examine those ideas by their roots!

3. **Be a possibility thinker.** Next time you're on a sinking ship loaded with squealing "hawgs," don't panic! Think about what can be done to get that ship successfully to its destination. If you are determined, you will find the way.

CHAPTER 4:

YOU'RE NOT A LEADER UNLESS···

....

Lincoln's Logs, by Gene Griessman

My family left Indiana in 1830 and moved to a farm near Decatur, Illinois. Soon afterward, I left home and became a clerk in New Salem, Illinois, a short-lived village located about seven miles from Springfield.

In 1832, having nothing better to do, several of my New Salem neighbors and I formed a company of volunteers, and marched off to serve in the Black Hawk War.[2] Each company was required to choose its own officers, and on the day before we were to join up with the other companies, we held an election.

One of my friends nominated me for captain. The other candidate was a man by the name of William Kirkpatrick, a businessman from New Salem. I had once worked for this man. He had cheated me out of some wages, and my friends knew it.

Our company made its choice in a dramatic manner. By agreement, Kirkpatrick and I walked away from the group and stood facing the men until a signal was given.

---

2 A conflict between an Illinois militia, called up by then-Governor John Reynolds, and a group of Sac and Fox Indians led by Black Hawk. These Native Americans had lived in Illinois before losing their property in a disputed treaty signed in 1804. In 1832, they decided to reclaim their land, but were eventually routed at Bad Axe on the Mississippi River. Source: http://lincoln.lib.niu.edu/blackhawk/

The men were told, if they wanted Kirkpatrick to be captain, to line up with him, and if they wanted me to be captain, to line up with me. Then the signal was given. The election was over in a matter of seconds. A few men walked over to join Kirkpatrick, but over two-thirds of them lined up with me.

That early success gave me more pleasure than any I have had since. It was my first political victory.

I learned a great deal about leadership from that experience. You're not a leader—unless you can get people to follow you. You may shout about being a leader all day long, but if nobody will listen to you, you're just fooling yourself.

In New Salem, I became a champion wrestler—one of the best on the frontier. I worked as a bargeman, as a surveyor, thought about becoming a blacksmith, read my first law book, became a partner in a grocery, went bankrupt, met and fell in love with Ann Rutledge, had a nervous breakdown, was a member of a debating society, served as postmaster, was elected to the Illinois legislature, taught myself law, and was admitted to the bar. I know that's a mouthful, but I was trying to find my way, find something I could be really good at.

Looking back, I now realize that all these varied experiences equipped me for leadership—for knowing what people thought and felt and for knowing how to appeal to them.

When I was twenty-eight years old, I moved from New Salem, which had begun to die, to the growing city of Springfield, which became the state capital. There I began to practice law, first, as a junior partner of John T. Stuart, and four years later as partner of Stephen T. Logan—both able lawyers who taught me a great deal.

Abraham Lincoln had the self-confidence and moral courage to make difficult decisions and to stand behind them and accept the consequences.

- GERALD PROKOPOWICZ,
CIVIL WAR EXPERT, AUTHOR, AND HOST OF CIVIL WAR TALK RADIO

Much of my law business came from riding the Eighth Judicial Circuit, where I rode with other lawyers and a judge, going from one county courthouse to the next, often for weeks at a time. Eventually I formed the law firm of Lincoln & Herndon, which continued until my death.

In Springfield, I made lasting friendships and met Mary Todd, whom I married in 1842. Four sons were born to us in Springfield: Robert, Edward (Eddie, we called him), William (Willie, we called him), and Thomas, whom we nicknamed "Tad." Eddie died in Springfield, of a fever.

In Springfield I was elected, as a member of the Whig Party, to serve one term in Congress, where I opposed the Mexican War—a decision I felt was right, but which almost ended my political career.

Springfield was like a magnet in those days, attracting some of the finest legal and political minds in America. I made it my business to associate with them, study them, learn from them, bind them to me, as Shakespeare said, with hoops of steel.

Springfield was where I lived when I engaged in the debates with Stephen Douglas, debates about the spread of slavery.

Springfield was where I lived when I left the Whig Party to become a Republican—a party that was formed to prevent the spread of slavery into the western territories. We Republicans were the radicals and liberals of our day.

Springfield was where I lived when I was elected President of the United States.

When I left Springfield for Washington in 1860, a crowd of about a thousand people assembled in the rain at the train station for an emotional farewell. I was asked to say a few words, and this is what I said:

"My friends—no one, not in my situation, can appreciate my feeling of sadness at this parting. To this place, and the kindness of these people, I owe everything. Here I have lived a quarter of a century, and have passed from a young to an old man. Here my children have been born and one is buried. I now leave, not knowing when, or whether ever, I may return— with a task before me greater than that which rested upon Washington. Without the assistance of the Divine Providence who ever attended him, I cannot succeed. With that assistance I cannot fail. Trusting in Him, who can go with me, and remain with you and be everywhere for good, let us confidently hope that all will yet be well. To His care commending you, as I hope in your prayers you will commend me, I bid you an affectionate farewell."

I never returned to Springfield until my body was brought back to be buried there.

Much has been written about Lincoln's failures. It is true that Abraham Lincoln had plenty of failures...in romance and business and politics...but Lincoln had many successes....
As a lawyer, Lincoln tried over 5,000 cases. He did not win all of them, but enough to make him famous.

— GENE GRIESSMAN

Taking a Stand Against Friends
for the Good of All

In the 1800s, Presidents were not inaugurated until March, long months after the election in November. In the days following my election, the country lurched toward civil war. Representatives from the states of the Deep South met in Montgomery, Alabama, and voted to secede from the Union.

On my inaugural trip to Washington there was a plot to assassinate me in Baltimore, but we learned of it, and I slipped into Washington in disguise. It was not an auspicious beginning.

I chose a cabinet of the most able men I could find, regardless of their political party or whether or not they admired me.

I knew that my inaugural address would be my last chance, my very last chance, to try to persuade my Southern friends not to leave the Union. Here is how I concluded that speech:

"My countrymen, one and all, think calmly and well, upon this whole subject. Nothing valuable can be lost by taking time....In your hands, my dissatisfied fellow countrymen, and not in mine, is the momentous issue of civil war. The government will not assail you. You can have no conflict, without being yourselves the aggressors. You have no oath registered in Heaven to destroy the government, while I shall have the most solemn one to 'preserve, protect and defend' it.

I am loathe to close. We are not enemies, but friends. We must not be enemies. Though passion may have strained, it must not break our bonds of affection. The mystic chords of memory, stretching from every battle-field, and patriot grave, to every living heart and hearthstone, all over this broad land, will yet swell the chorus of the Union, when again touched, as surely they will be, by the better angels of our nature."

And the war came.

Two long, sad years later I wrote these words:

> "*Fellow-citizens, we cannot escape history. We of this Congress and this administration will be remembered in spite of ourselves. No personal significance, or insignificance, can spare one or another of us.*
>
> *The fiery trial through which we pass will light us down, in honor or dishonor, to the latest generation. We say we are for the Union. The world will not forget that we say this. We know how to save the Union. The world knows we do know how to save it. We—even we here—hold the power, and bear the responsibility.*
>
> *In giving freedom to the slave, we assure freedom to the free—honorable alike in what we give, and what we preserve. We shall nobly save, or meanly lose, the last best hope of earth.*
>
> *Other means may succeed; this could not fail. The way is plain, peaceful, generous, just—a way which, if followed, the world will forever applaud, and God must forever bless.*"

---

*While pretending no indifference to earthly honors, I **do** claim to be actuated in this contest by something higher than an anxiety for office.*

– A. LINCOLN

Living Lincoln: Leaders are Principled

By Pat Williams

Leaders who fail to develop and live by principles are leaders whose names are often ultimately forgotten. Standing up for what is right may cost you, but in the long run I believe right will prevail. So why not be on the winning side, long term?

Springfield, at that time, was a magnet for great minds and Lincoln chose to spend his time with them, to study them and learn from them. He understood that every leader is a learner, and he knew that some of the best opportunities to learn came in relationship to other bright individuals. So he cultivated relationships with the finest minds of his time. We can all learn to lead like Lincoln if we'll take hold of this lesson. Yes, Springfield was a center of activity in Lincoln's day, but we don't really need to move to the intellectual centers to find people who can inspire us. The world today is ripe with such opportunities—in the workplace, at our schools, in books, and even on the Internet. Who can you learn from? Get to know those people well. Lincoln did.

Few things shape the minds and skills of leaders better than open debating. It's where we learn to articulate and defend our positions on various issues. Debating isn't done as often as it once was, but it is not by any means dead.

Since Lincoln's day, in fact, presidential debates have become a much-anticipated part of the American political landscape. We can count on them, every four years, and they are all nationally televised. So important have these events become that they can literally make or break a person's desire to sit in the Oval Office.

What seems lacking today is the civility that once characterized these verbal contests. But we can change that—as Lincoln said of saving the Union, we know the way. We can choose to participate in or benefit from the debate format. Well-argued points-of-view lead to a more balanced society. Let's be leaders who aren't ashamed or afraid to argue persuasively for what we believe and know to be right.

It was also in Springfield where Lincoln left the Whig Part to join the newly forming Republican Party, created to stop the spread of slavery.

When you find yourself moving in a direction that no longer lines up with the group or organization with which you've been traveling, maybe it's time to re-examine their goals. Lincoln was fully persuaded that slavery was wrong. He was passionate about stopping it! But where were the Whig voices? His party was deeply divided over this hot button issue. So Lincoln left the party and ultimately stacked hands with those whose early slogan was, in part, "free soil, free labor, free speech, free men."

Where do you see a wrong direction that needs to be averted? Lead like Lincoln and have the courage to do what it takes to stem the tide.

One day in 1860, about a thousand people gathered to wish Mr. Lincoln a fond and tearful farewell as he left his Springfield, Illinois home and made his way to Washington, D.C. Lincoln was a citizen of his community. People knew him.

Leaders are people who make themselves known, accessible, and available to others. Lead like Lincoln by being authentic. Get to know those you lead and make sure they know you too.

President-elect Lincoln acknowledged the burden that rested on his shoulders and the need for reliance on Divine Providence—he knew that trusting in God, he could not fail.

What burden are you shouldering on your own? Why not unload it right now. I'm not talking about getting religious—don't worry! But I am talking about recognizing that which we all know at our core—we are not here by accident. Each one of us is created for a unique time, place, and purpose. How much less stressful our lives become when, like Abraham

Lincoln, we learn to call on the Divine Providence that placed us here in the first place. Many times in my own life and career, I've called on God and I've seen him come through when my own efforts were completely spent. I believe he wants us to do that, and long before we reach the end of our ropes.

Lincoln Lessons for Today
Wisdom to Apply Right Now

1. **Ask yourself every morning, "From whom can I learn today?"** Maybe it's the driver who runs the shuttle bus from the train station to your office, or the young intern you just took on board—or it could even be your boss. Each person in your life has the capacity to teach you something about life, if you'll open your eyes, ears, and heart to the lesson.

2. When choosing a team of advisers—whether in a business situation or simply a team of people with whom to "do life"—**don't look for only those who agree with you** or who sympathize with your decisions no matter what. Be like Lincoln and choose those who are the most able, those who will enhance your life in any direction.

3. Remember Lincoln at the Springfield station, surrounded by people who knew him. **Be a leader who is known to those you lead**—an active member of your community.

CHAPTER 5:

WHAT HAPPENED AT GETTYSBURG — AND WHY IT MATTERS TODAY

....

Lincoln's Logs, by Gene Griessman

During the darkest days of the Civil War, one of my supporters recommended that I find an appropriate occasion to tell the nation why we were fighting this bloody war. What was the purpose of this staggering loss of treasure and lives?

Not long afterwards, I received an invitation to participate in the dedication of the military cemetery at Gettysburg. I accepted with this goal in mind. It would be my opportunity to tell, in plain language, what I thought was the main aim of the war.

It was my deeply felt belief that the war was not just about ending slavery or saving the union, as vital as those objectives were. What was at stake was the future of democracy—the future of people's government.

It was widely believed at the time that common, ordinary people were not capable of ruling themselves, that they must be ruled by kings and queens and generals and aristocrats.

With the coming of the Civil War the great American experiment, which was just a few decades old, was about to end just like all previous republics—by destroying itself. Discontented warring factions would tear it apart.

It was widely held that a republic is a weak form of government—too weak to survive for very long. John Adams observed that all republics eventually commit suicide.

When the Civil War began, it was really a struggle between two confederacies, one in the North and one in the South. The former colonies had experimented first with the Articles of Confederation, which left the states as little sovereign powers, much like little nations. That first experiment failed miserably, and a more centralized arrangement was created. But it was still, to all intents and purposes, a confederacy. In fact, I did not even call the United States a "nation" in my first Inaugural Address. I called it a "union."

I realized that the federal government was not strong enough to survive, that it needed to be more centralized, that the federal government was too weak, that the United States needed to become a nation in order to survive.

This great contest has been visibly held in the hands of Almighty God, and is a fulfillment of the solemn prophecies with which the Bible is sown thick as stars, that He would spare the soul of the needy, and judge the cause of the poor. It was He who chose the instrument for this work, and He chose him with a visible reference to the rights and interest of the great majority of mankind, for which he stood.

– HARRIET BEECHER STOWE,
FROM HER BOOK *MEN OF OUR TIMES*, HARTFORD PUBLISHING CO., 1868

Prior to my administration, the United States was referred to in the plural—"the United States *are*." After my administration, the United States began to be referred to in the singular, "the United States *is*." Some historians and political scientists have called this the most significant change that I produced in America. They may be correct in that particular assessment.

I felt that if people's government could not survive in America, where it was protected by wide oceans from the great, centralized powers of the world, that people's government could not survive anywhere.

Gettysburg would be my chance to tell the nation what was at stake.

The speech was short. But it was just the right length for the news-papers. The New York *Times* ran the entire Gettysburg Address on the front page.

There's a myth that I composed the Gettysburg Address on the back of an envelope on the way to the cemetery. It is not true. I had thought about the speech, and worked on it for days. You don't think I made a long trip from Washington to Gettysburg to say something off the cuff do you? People who think that don't know me at all. It *is* true that I was revising the speech, and polishing it, and trying to make it better on the way to the cemetery.

America and the Right to an Equal Chance

When I was a young man, I had come upon a profound idea written by Thomas Jefferson in the Declaration of Independence. It was one compact sentence. "All men are created equal." It was a radical thought at the time, and still is. I am not sure that you believe it today. It is counter-intuitive.

What did Jefferson mean when he wrote, "All men are created equal"? Jefferson was one of the most intelligent men who ever lived. He could look around him and see that all are not born equal in height or weight. All are not equal in intelligence or athletic ability. All are not equal in musical ability. I'm about like one of my generals who told me, "Lincoln, I can recognize just two songs: One is 'Yankee Doodle,' and the other one isn't."

What did Jefferson mean, "All men are created equal"?

It was a political statement. He meant that all are born with the right to an equal chance.

You see, America is more than geography. America is more than majestic mountain peaks, endless rolling plains, wide beaches, and thundering seas.

America is a great experiment—an experiment in democratizing opportunity. America is the biggest experiment in the history of the world at giving all sorts of people a chance—a chance for this poor, awkward, semi-literate boy growing up on the frontier—a chance for me to become President. That couldn't have happened anywhere in the world at that time, except in America.

---

*I shall be most happy indeed if I should be an humble instrument
in the hands of the Almighty, and of this, his almost chosen
people, for perpetuating the object of that great struggle.*

– A . L I N C O L N ,
IN A SPEECH MADE EN ROUTE TO HIS INAUGURATION

And just like Thomas Jefferson, I embedded that same idea in the words I spoke at Gettysburg.

The principal speaker of the day was a great orator by the name of Edward Everett. He spoke for two hours—a remarkable and beautiful address, entirely memorized.

They asked me to make "a few appropriate remarks." I think the emphasis was on few, perhaps to spare them and me an embarrassment.

I spoke for two minutes. And this is what I said at Gettysburg:

"Four score and seven years ago our fathers brought forth on this continent, a new nation, conceived in Liberty, and dedicated to the proposition that all men are created equal.

Now we are engaged in a great civil war, testing whether that nation, or any nation so conceived and so dedicated, can long endure. We are met on a great battlefield of that war. We have come to dedicate a portion of that field as a final resting place for those who here gave their lives that that nation might live. It is altogether fitting and proper that we should do this.

But in a larger sense we cannot dedicate, we cannot consecrate, we cannot hallow this ground. The brave men, living and dead, who struggled here, have consecrated it, far above our power to add or detract.

The world will little note, nor long remember what we say here, but it can never forget what they did here. It is for us the living, rather, to be dedicated here to the unfinished work which they who fought here have thus so far nobly advanced. It is rather for us to be here dedicated to the great task remaining before us—that from these honored dead we take increased devotion to that cause for which they here gave the last full measure of devotion; that we here highly resolve that these dead shall not have died in vain; that this nation, under God, shall have a new birth of freedom, and that government of the people, by the people, for the people, shall not perish from the earth."

Living Lincoln: Today's Gettysburg

By Pat Williams

Today, we might call it an "elevator speech"—your two-minute testimony. Abraham Lincoln had mastered the art of succinct communication long before we began teaching this concept in seminars, classrooms, and books. For Lincoln, the brief but concise and poetic Gettysburg Address summed up his thoughts on what America represented to history, and to the world. He recognized that there was, as there always is on most any issue, much disagreement among the citizenry regarding the motives, aims, and objectives of the Civil War. He used the Gettysburg Address as his opportunity to set the record straight. He realized that America's very survival hung in the balance.

What's at stake for your organization—your school, your team, your church, or your company? As leaders, we need to take advantage of every opportunity to go before our organizations and explain our actions or strategies. People respect and cooperate with a leader whose actions they understand. In my forty-seven years in professional sports, I've seen many times when a team fell apart before my eyes because of a failure to communicate strategy. By the same token, I have thrilled over teams, like our 1983 Philadelphia 76ers NBA championship squad, who understood each other's strengths and weaknesses so well their games were like a Tchaikovsky ballet on the court—beautifully choreographed and executed. There is just no substitute for clearly expressed goals and objectives and the results they obtain.

It is not enough to do your best; you must know
what to do, and THEN do your best.

— W. EDWARDS DEMING

Another quality we see here in Abraham Lincoln's leadership style is his belief that everyone deserved an equal chance to succeed at life and be heard.

Where in your organization do you need to give more voice to those you lead? One of the biggest marketplace complaints I hear is about leaders who micromanage. They just can't let go and delegate the work, trusting in those they've hired to get it right. I'll grant you that business is not meant to be a system of government, but surely neither are you out to be a dictator. I urge you to see yourself as both a leader and a mentor. After all, the best leaders come from within an organization, and for that to happen they must be allowed to stand on the shoulders of current leadership.

I was just twenty-four years old when I was given the phenomenal opportunity to operate my own ball club—the Spartanburg Phillies, a farm club of the Philadelphia Phillies. I didn't know it going in, but that job would become a building block for everything that came after it— thanks to the inspiring and exemplary leadership style of my boss, Spartanburg co-owner Mr. R.E. Littlejohn (the slow thinker of Chapter 3). So well-respected was this fine Southern gentleman that everyone in town called him "Mr. R.E."—including his wife!

On the night I first arrived in town, Mrs. Littlejohn said of her husband, "You'll never again work for another man like him. He's the greatest man in the world." It didn't take long for me to realize this was not just a wife's devotion speaking. Mr. R.E., or "Coach," as I later came to call him, was truly one in a million. He had an amazing way of making you completely comfortable in his presence—a great man whose greatness never overshadowed you. To Mr. R.E., you were on the same level.

But Mr. R.E. was a businessman, and he and his partner Leo Hughes had no time for sprucing up a ballpark—that's what they hired me for. As I steamed ahead full speed, I was amazed how Mr. R.E. kept in constant contact with me. He wasn't watching over my shoulder, making sure I was doing things just his way—no, not at all. Rather, he was telling me continually how much he believed in me and that he thought I was doing my job well. Was I? Probably not all the time, but Mr. R.E. sure made me feel that I was. Do you think that made any difference in my job performance? You had better believe it.

How can you, like Mr. R.E., inspire your direct reports? In what ways can you model treating everyone equally, as Abraham Lincoln so eloquently challenged us to do?

Lincoln spent many hours preparing his two-minute Gettysburg Address. How much time and thought do you put into the words you use when speaking to those you lead? Even our daily conversations can leave a lasting impact. If the message you're delivering matters, I encourage you to lead like Lincoln and think long and hard about what you're going to say. Then work on it and make it the best it can be. Don't be guilty of "off the cuff" remarks that may be misconstrued over the lunch table. Your goals may not be Gettysburgian in their lifespan, but if you believe they are worthwhile, then they deserve to be communicated with clarity and passion.

Lincoln Lessons for Today
Wisdom to Apply Right Now

1. **Let your actions reflect your faith.** Do you believe that all people should have an equal opportunity to succeed? Don't have one standard for your peers and another for your subordinates. I'm not talking about business standards—those, of course, will be different based on job level, experience, and expectations. But in your relationships with others, whoever they are, be fair and be consistent.

2. **Give everyone an equal chance.** Lincoln said America is an experiment in giving all kinds of people a chance—and 200 years after Lincoln's birth, more than 230 from our nation's birth—it's an experiment that is succeeding. To whom do you need to give a chance? Think about that— and then think about how you will go about extending that opportunity.

3. **Communicate your message clearly.** As much as it is in your power, make sure everyone on your team understands your message. In Lincoln's day we did not have 24/7 cable news with ample opportunity for viewpoints to be aired and scrutinized. Today, our ability and our opportunity to communicate is virtually unlimited. Use it wisely and well.

4. **Study your organization.** Look for any internal flaws, inherent contradictions, and systemic problems. W. Edwards Deming, father of the quality movement, focused on making the system work. That's what every successful leader has to do: make the system work. A faulty system will pull good workers down and an effective system will enable even mediocre workers to perform at high levels.

5. **Try to make your organization stronger.** Great major-league baseball teams often are great because they have a great farm system to draw from—a place where beginners can grow so the team can be stronger and more effective. Lincoln realized that a loose confederacy had inherent problems and could not survive for very long. A weak confederacy certainly would be no match for the great centralized European powers that were eager to take over the New World. So he set about to make the federal government stronger and to function more effectively. This, by the way, is one of Lincoln's most important contributions to the U.S. and to the world.

CHAPTER 6:

SUCCESS COMES FROM WITHIN

....

Lincoln's Logs, by Gene Griessman

I attribute whatever success I may have had to discovering, and observing, some basic principles of success and achievement. We can call them secrets of success, if you wish, for, although they seem obvious once you see them, millions of people pass through life seemingly unaware that these principles exist. Perhaps they are secrets, after all. I believe that if you do these things, your life will be full of achievements.

Let's start with the most important principle of success. Here it is:

If you want to be successful at anything, you must *will* that success into existence.

Success comes from within. Success is something you do with your will, your head, and your heart.

• *The ability to succeed depends on the strength of your own determination.*

You understand that somehow, some way, you will get there. You understand that even if you encounter setbacks, roadblocks, misunderstandings, and opposition, you will get there. Why? Because you have resolved that you will succeed.

You must not wait to be brought forward by the older men....
Do you suppose that I should ever have got into notice if I had
waited to be hunted up and pushed forward by older men?

— A . L I N C O L N

When I was young, I read a book that most people read in my day, but few read today—*Pilgrim's Progress*, by John Bunyan. It's a classic that tells the story of a lonely, resolute traveler who struggled with temptation, overcame despondency, and reached his goal. *Pilgrim's Progress* became a metaphor for my life.

• *Everything flows from your will, builds upon it, grows out of it, is propelled by it.*

Great religious leaders have long taught that if you truly want something, you should act as if the object of your desire is already on its way to you. For example, if your goal is to become a lawyer, visualize yourself as a lawyer, and you will be well on your way to achieving that dream. *Seeing* it happen is the way to *make* it happen.

• *Will power is a thought that is held deeply enough and long enough to produce action.*

I think I already told you that I was a wrestler, and a good one. I learned that you don't win a fight simply going though the motions. You win by resolving that you will win. If you get thrown down, you figure out a way to win the next time, maybe with a different hold or a different position.

During the War, I wrote a personal letter to a college student who was a friend of my son Robert. His grades were bad, he was discouraged, and he was considering dropping out of college. In that letter I said, "You cannot fail if you resolutely determine that you will not."

This principle may sound too mystical for you, and some of the things that happen to you after you will something into existence may seem uncanny. But I assure you that this principle has practical, down-to-earth applications.

A businessman once told me about one of his salesmen. This particular salesmen had not made his quota, and the owner of the company was concerned about him.

"Are you going to let him go?" I asked. "No."

"Why not?" I asked.

"The man has drive," the owner replied. I understood immediately.

Drive is another word for resolution, for will power.

If you make even a cursory study of the great leaders of history in any field, you will discover that they did not get to be leaders by wishing it, but by willing it. They all—good and bad—had strong wills. In the field of art, of which I know little, I am told that great painters force the world to see nature the way they see it.

- *Get in the habit of succeeding with the tasks that you choose.*

Choose your tasks carefully. Choose what's worth doing. And then go at it with complete determination. "Must" is the word.

This is not to say that there will not be failures on your way to eventual success. That was certainly true in my life. But I always believed that if a thing was worth doing, I would find a way to do it.

When I made up my mind to be President, when I was very young, there is no way that I could have imagined that success would mean presiding over a civil war, and emancipating the slaves, and saving the Union.

Looking back over my life, it was my resolution to succeed that made the difference.

The great quality of his appearance was benevolence and benignity: the wish to do somebody some good if he could.

– CHARLES DANA, LINCOLN'S
ASSISTANT SECRETARY OF WAR

Living Lincoln: See Yourself Successful
By Pat Williams

This is a message I believe in wholeheartedly. I've seen it happen time after time after time. Why do homerun hitters drive the ball into the bleacher seats? Because they see it happen before the wood connects with the leather. Keep your eyes on the prize. That, my friends, is what it takes to succeed.

Where are you feeling discouraged? What vision seems just out of reach for you? Have faith in what you believe should happen. Faith, the Scripture says, is the evidence of things not seen. Like the main character in *Pilgrim's Progress*, Lincoln explains, life is filled with numerous difficulties. Everything flows from the will. If you truly want something, Lincoln says, echoing the words of religious leaders throughout the ages, you should act as if the object of your desires is already on its way to you. Will power, according to Lincoln, is a thought held deeply and long enough to produce action. You win by resolving that you will win. Like Lincoln, I believe we all want to say, "Looking back over my life, it was my resolution to succeed that made the difference."

"If you can force your heart and nerve and sinew
To serve your turn long after they are gone,
And so hold on when there is nothing in you
Except the Will which says to them: 'Hold on';

...If you can fill the unforgiving minute
With sixty seconds' worth of distance run -
Yours is the Earth and everything that's in it,
And - which is more - you'll be a Man my son!

"IF," BY RUDYARD KIPLING

Jim Brown, the legendary Cleveland Browns running back, was the first athlete I ever heard talk about visioning this way. The night before games he would think about what he wanted to accomplish, picture it as if he'd already done it. When game time came, his mission was already half accomplished. Because he'd seen himself successful, the doing of it was simply the living out of history.

Mark Price, who is among the greatest free throw shooters in NBA history, constantly visualized the ball going into the basket in advance of the games. After repeatedly playing the scene over and over in his mind, by game time it was all automatic.

I ran across a quote from golfer Vijay Singh that further illustrates this amazing power our minds hold. Singh said, "My unconscious mind had a lot of stored up bad thoughts in there and that was the key, to get rid of all that. I just tell to myself, 'I'm the best putter on the planet" (*USA Today*, September 24, 2008).

In his book *Time Tactics of Very Successful People* (McGraw-Hill, Inc., 1994), Gene Griessman writes about his Georgia Tech colleague Homer

C. Rice—college athletic director and a football coach who, over his career, compiled a record that is nothing short of astonishing. Rice's secret was his passion for excellence. He devoured books on achievement and wrote out his goals on three by five cards. Everywhere he went, he took those cards with him, reading them over and over to press them into his subconscious.

That system is one I also adopted many years ago. When I come up with great stories, quotes, Bible verses, etc., I have them typed on both sides of 3x5 cards. Then I laminate the cards, and carry them with me when I'm travelling, jogging, or waiting in line. Thanks to that habit, all of those nuggets are tucked away somewhere in the back of my mind, ready to be called up whenever I speak to a group. It's a wonderful practice for being ready at a moment's notice anytime you need a story or illustration to help you make a point. I recommend it.

The mind is so powerful. What we think about all day long ultimately is going to become reality in our lives. Our brain is a computer beyond comparison. To create a computer that could do everything our brain does, it would have to be twenty-two stories tall and as big as Dallas, Texas.

So many people who are successful in life set themselves up for success by refusing to let negative thoughts get into their thinking pattern in any way. They deliberately disassociate themselves from the people Walt Disney called well-poisoners, those who are always negative.

In my reading, writing, and study of success, I've discovered that the first foundational block is always that of thinking successful thoughts. Every good deed, every charitable effort, every hospital, every great university, started out as a tiny thought in someone's mind. By the same token, every act of evil, every murder, every war—started in the mind of some man or woman. Both good and evil begin in the mind and then those thoughts become actions.

So the more I plow through life, the more I find that right thinking and the deliberate feeding into your mind of the right stuff, is what determines the course of your life—every time, without exception.

Lincoln Lessons for Today
Wisdom to Apply Right Now

1. **Success begins in the head and the heart.** Determine with your mind and establish in your heart that you will succeed at your chosen life goal—in fact, at *all* of them!

2. **Remember that everything begins with will power.** You will yourself to win! Lincoln lived by this quote from Benjamin Franklin: "Resolve to perform what you ought; perform without fail what you resolve." Try it yourself and let me know what happens.

3. **Where do you want to succeed?** Picture it as having already happened. Like Jim Brown, picture yourself moving down the field and scoring that touchdown—big as life, in high definition. Then when it happens, it will be like watching an instant replay.

CHAPTER 7:

HOW TO LEARN BY LISTENING

··

Lincoln's Logs, by Gene Griessman

I had only one year of schooling, but I had a lifelong education… because I *learned* how to learn. After all is said and done, you don't *get* an education—you *learn* how to learn. This sounds so easy that you may be tempted to say to yourself, "I'm already doing that." But are you?

Here's a way to determine if you've learned how to learn. If you were to meet somebody today whom you haven't seen for, say, five years, would that person be able to detect any difference in you? Would you seem more knowledgeable to them, wiser? Would they be able to tell others that you seem better informed, more competent, more self-possessed than you were when they last saw you?

If you learn how to learn, you will be different in important ways five years from today.

Listen

We're born with the ability to see, but we have to learn how to read. We're born with the ability to hear, but we have to learn how to listen.

- *Before you tell, ask. Before you speak, listen. Listen intently.*

Most of the time, most people listen, on a ten-point scale, at about a three or four. Hence, a lot of valuable information slips right past them.

You can raise your level of listening intensity to nines and tens on a ten-point scale through an act of the will, and you can sustain that high level through practice and discipline. Listen totally. If it's a face-to-face conversation, learn to read the speaker's face. Listen with your eyes, not just your ears.

Many people use their faces as masks. They put on the mask they think is most appropriate for a particular situation. If it's a sad occasion, they put on a mournful face. If it's a joyous occasion, they put on a happy face—because it's the face that's expected. But sometimes people will drop their masks, perhaps for just a moment, and reveal what they truly think and feel.

Even after Lincoln became a successful lawyer, he did most of his reading out loud, much to the annoyance of his law partner William Herndon. Lincoln told one of his law clerks, "I write by ear. When I have put my thoughts on paper, I read it aloud, and if it sounds all right, I just let it pass."

– DOUGLAS L. WILSON,
FROM *LINCOLN'S SWORD: THE PRESIDENCY AND THE POWER OF WORDS* (ALFRED A. KNOPF 2006)

Listen to what is **not** said—to what they do not say when they have an opportunity to say it.

• *Listen attentively, especially to people who disagree with you.*

Your first impulse will be to try to convince them they're wrong and you're right. But if you listen attentively you gain the advantage, because you know their argument as well as your own. My senior law partner taught me, "Lincoln, when you're going to try a case, think more about what your opponent is going to say than what you're going to say."

You may have heard about my debates with Stephen Douglas. Those debates attracted tens of thousands of people. Douglas by that time was a U.S. Senator, a national figure. I was just a regionally known lawyer. He was one of the best debaters and shrewdest orators this nation has ever produced. The only way I was able to hold my own with Stephen Douglas was that I anticipated his arguments. I spent a lot of time thinking about what he was going to say and listening to how he said it. I listened and I listened. I was totally there—and that enabled me to know what response to make, what story to tell in order to give a good accounting of myself.

• *Listen to continue your education. Everybody you meet knows more than you do about something.*

If you're attentive and patient, and do more than small talk, you can draw this out of them.

You can always learn something. Think of the people around you as pages of your encyclopedia. You can turn a page at almost anytime and increase your knowledge. Others will be flattered that you're interested in them and you will be the wiser for it.

Living Lincoln: Learn to Learn by Listening
by Pat Williams

Learning how to learn—by listening to others—is one of the most critical lessons I can think of in this day of constantly diverted attention. We are continually being distracted by the noise around us, and it keeps us from really hearing anything at all. If this lesson of learning to listen to others was difficult in Lincoln's time, how much more is it for us today?

Think back to your childhood. How many times did you hear a teacher or parent say, "Are you listening to me?" At first, that question usually meant a punishment of some kind was on its way. But as you got older, the wise teacher or parent let you suffer your own consequences for failing to listen—a relationship that got you in trouble or a poor grade on the term final, perhaps.

As adults, the consequences of failing to listen can mean personal, national, or even international disaster. We may invest poorly and lose our shirts, or vote poorly and lose our liberties. In the workplace, failing to listen can cost us a promotion or even a job. In marriage, I don't want to tell you what failing to listen can mean. Perhaps you already know. It is not a pretty story.

So what can we do to get to that nine or ten on the listening scale, as Lincoln suggests? There are many creative ideas, and I'm sure you can come up with your own. Here are a few suggestions:

- **Take notes.** Lincoln talked about listening intently while Douglas spoke. He majored in Douglas by studying the man. Whose arguments do you need to refute? Take notes when they talk and then think about how your position is different. This is easiest to do when you're in an audience listening to a speaker, but however it is accomplished, I recommend it.

- **Determine not to talk or even interject a comment while the other person is speaking.** At first, this may be difficult—especially when that perfect comeback springs to your mind. But when you make it an object of your will, as Lincoln says, you'll find that in time you'll get better and better at doing it. In time, you'll find yourself listening—because you want to! You'll discover that the person who is talking is really interesting. Sometimes we find ourselves assailed by people who love to talk. If you are quiet by nature and often find yourself on the receiving end of a person who doesn't know the meaning of "stop," ask yourself if maybe that person has a need to talk—and maybe you have a need to listen. It's easy in such circumstances to think, "Well, why doesn't *he* listen sometimes? Why do *I* always have to be the one who does the listening?" I urge you to use these moments as opportunities for personal growth, rather than brewing up barrels of bitterness. Often you will find that if you listen attentively and silently without interrupting the other person, they eventually will pause and ask: "What do you think?" or "Do you agree?" That is the cue for your input.

- **Recognize that there are more points of view than just yours.** We have a natural tendency—made more obvious in our polarized political climate—to dismiss the arguments of people with whom we disagree. I believe that's a mistake. We are a world of optimists and pessimists for a reason—because somewhere in the middle is the proper balance. The wise leader listens to other perspectives, for at least two reasons: 1) to show respect and willingness to consider another point of view, and 2) to listen for the weaknesses to help build her own argument for another side.

- **Be willing to learn from those who've gone before you.** In the '70s, there was a popular song by Billy Joel that said, "I don't care what you say, this is my life." It's a universal theme among the young, as I can attest after raising nineteen fiercely independent souls (see chapter 11). And just as universally, if we're honest with ourselves, we eventually learn that we should have cared about that advice, whatever it may have been. We live in an era where "rights" trump the common, or even the individual, good. Yet who is hurt when we fail to listen to our parents, our teachers, or anyone who's been down the road upon which we are traveling and knows well its potholes? You and I, my friend. We are the ones who later nurse our wounded pride and ice pack our bruised egos. The wise person learns from the mistakes of others. We learn by listening.

I find it interesting that the words "listen" and "silent" are made up of the same letters. I think there's a message tucked in there somewhere. When I speak to business leaders, often I ask, rhetorically, "Have you ever worked for a company where you heard this complaint about the CEO: 'If that woman would just give up that endless listening she does around here, maybe this company would get somewhere,' or 'All the president of this company ever does is listen to us. It's destroying this company'?" And then I chuckle and say, "You've never heard that. And you never will."

Lincoln Lessons for Today

Wisdom to Apply Right Now

1. **Determine to be a good listener.** That means being *silent* when someone else is speaking!

2. **Pay attention to who is speaking**, and note what they say.

3. **Don't interrupt!** Most of us like to speak our minds and be heard, to get a complete thought out before we are jumped on or cut off. Yes, there are times for making points, asking questions, or cutting off an overly loquacious individual, but as a general rule, avoid interrupting whenever possible.

4. **Learn to listen reflexively** in conversations, making sure you understand what is being said by saying (when it's your turn to speak) something like, "Let me make sure I understand what you're saying" and then attempt to rephrase the first speaker's main points.

5. **Sit back and be amazed by how much you learn!**

*I made it a rule to forbear all direct Contradiction to the Sentiments of others, and all positive Assertion of my own. I even forbid myself agreeable to the old Laws of our Junto, the Use of every Word or Expression in the Language that **imported a fix'd Opinion;** such as certainly, undoubtedly, &c. and I adopted instead of them, I conceive, I apprehend, or I imagine a thing to be so or so, or it so appears to me at present. When another asserted something, that I though an Error, I deny'd myself the Pleasure of contradicting him abruptly, and of showing immediately some Absurdity in his Proposition; and in answering I began by observing that in certain Cases or Circumstances his Opinion would be right, but that in the present case there appear'd or seem'd to me some Difference, &c.…. And to this Habit (after my Character of Integrity) I think it principally owing, that I had early so much Weight with my Fellow Citizens, when I proposed new Institutions, or Alterations in the old; and so much Influence in public Councils when I became a Member. For I was but a bad Speaker, never eloquent, subject to much Hesitation in my choice of Words, hardly correct in Language, and yet I generally carried my Points.*

BENJAMIN FRANKLIN,
AUTOBIOGRAPHY, SECTION 39 ITALICS ADDED

CHAPTER 8:

HOW TO LEARN BY READING

....

Lincoln's Logs, by Gene Griessman

When I was just a youngster it dawned on me that reading was a key to a roomful of treasure. Inside that room was the accumulated knowledge of those who had come before me—a roomful of treasure, just waiting to be taken. All I had to do was turn the key and open the door.

At first, I was a general reader. I read everything I could put my hands on. By the time I left Indiana at the age of twenty, I'd read practically every book within a radius of fifty miles. You say, "Well, there weren't many books then." I know. But there were some. And I'd read them.

There are *two kinds of reading that make for success*:

- One will launch your journey.

- The other will help you complete it.

The first kind of reading is general reading, the kind of reading I did in Indiana and to a lesser extent all my life. If you're a general reader, you'll eventually know a little about a lot of things. This kind of knowledge will make your life more interesting and it will enable you to carry on conversations with a wide range of people. But general reading has limitations. In fact, general reading can become a time-waster, a distraction, a diversion.

So let me say a few words about **the second kind of reading. It is focused, in-depth reading.** Instead of staying on the surface, you drill deep.

In-depth reading is a way to become an expert, and that is a *powerful success principle.* Obviously, not all knowledge has the same value, but amazingly, you can make a mark in the world if you become an expert on virtually any subject, if you become known as the person that people go to about a subject. Shortly after I moved to New Salem I discovered in-depth reading. I acquired a set of Blackstone's Commentaries on the Laws of England and began to study them. A fire began to burn inside me as I pored over the pages. It was hard reading for someone with barely a year of schooling, but I kept at it.

At that time I was working at a general store, and one day I was off in the corner of the store with my book. A friend walked in and asked me what I was reading. I told him, "I'm not reading. I'm studying." There's a big difference.

This principle of studying through focused, in-depth reading was one I could use anywhere. Just get me the books.

---

*Lincoln learned to read in little schools on the frontier
that were called "blab schools." These schools got
their name from the common practice of requiring
students to recite their lessons out loud.*

– GENE GRIESSMAN

When I was practicing law in Springfield, I took a patent-infringement case that would be tried before the state supreme court. When I got the case, I approached an architect I knew and asked him to order the best books on the subject from New York and Chicago.

After they arrived, one night each week we met and my architect friend tutored me from those books. Later when I tried the case and made a good showing, the other lawyers said, "I didn't know Lincoln knew anything about that." I didn't—not when I started out.

In my forties, Billy Herndon asked me one day if I could "prove" a point. I asked him what he meant by *prove*. Billy replied, "*Prove*, as in a mathematical proof."

I knew little about mathematics, so I asked him how I could learn to do mathematical proofs. Billy told me to read Euclid. I obtained a copy of Euclid's Elements—thirteen small books in all—and took it with me on the judicial circuit. After the other lawyers had gone to sleep, I would stay up and study Euclid.

From that time on, observers began to say that my speeches had moved to a new level. I'd learned to combine the power of a mathematical proof with the power of emotion.

I continued to do in-depth reading after I became President. I checked out books from the Library of Congress on military strategy so that I could understand what the generals and admirals were doing. That study did not equip me to be a great general or a great admiral, but it did enable me to ask good questions and carry on intelligent conversations with generals and admirals.

Get the books and read and study them in their principal features; and that is the main thing. The books, and your capacity for understanding them, are just the same in all places.

— A. LINCOLN,
ADVICE TO AN ASPIRING LAWYER

Living Lincoln: Leaders Are Readers
by Pat Williams

Learning how to learn through books is without a doubt my personal choice—and one I engage in vigorously every day. Those who know me will tell you it's rare to see me without a book in my hands. I've made it a personal goal to finish at least one book a day, with several others in progress. "A book a day!" you say. I admit I'm a bit unusual on that score, but I've learned it can be done.

Years ago after a speaking engagement in Charleston, South Carolina I met a woman named Margaret Cotton, who'd spent fifteen years teaching speed-reading for the Evelyn Wood speed reading schools so popular in the 1950s and '60s. She told me that the average person has the potential to read seven-hundred-and-fifty words per minute—more if you're reading in your field of interest. As an avid reader even back then, I was stunned. I asked her if she would share a few tips with me and I took good notes. Here are her tips, in a nutshell. May they transform your reading life as they have mine:

1. **Use your finger or a pen to keep your eyes focused on the page.** Typically our eyes wander as we read and we lose focus. Using a pointer in this way keeps your eyes focused on the page.

2. **Read fast.** You do that by practicing. At first you won't get it all, but that's OK. Keep working at it. You'll find in time that your brain is able to absorb information at a much faster rate than your eye. Retention will come as you practice.

3. **Use your full field of vision.** Your eyes can take in far more than one word at a time. Use your peripheral vision and grab words in chunks, first in phrases and then in sentences

until you work up to paragraphs. The object is to get those words from your eyes to your brain quickly. This may not always work for pleasure reading, but it's remarkably effective when getting information is your goal.

I am eternally grateful for the "chance" meeting with Ms. Cotton.

Good tips for remembering what you've read involve writing it down. Quiz yourself afterwards with questions like, "What was the author's main point?" or write down the three key take-away lessons from the chapter. Writing book reviews on Amazon or simply telling your friends, family, or co-workers about the book you just finished are great ways to remember. Put what you read to work for you as soon as possible after reading.

Leaders are readers—have you heard that phrase before? It's true! No matter what position you are in, someone has been there before. And at least one of them has written a book on their experiences. Learn from them. Build on their foundation. Make it your own and establish a legacy of your own—one that might have you writing a book of your own for that next generation…the one coming up right behind you.

Lincoln understood the value of an education gained through books. Wherever you left off when you graduated from college, I imagine you'll admit by now that you don't know everything. You may even have days where you wish you knew more. For goodness sake, don't leave it at that! You can know more tomorrow than you know today—by taking my reading challenge. Let me present it to you here:

- **Read for one hour a day, from a book.** Reports, newspapers, and magazines don't count! This is not just about exercising your eyes—it's about that in-depth learning Lincoln loved so much. It doesn't matter how you do that hour: you can do it all at once, or split it up any way that works for you—in two thirty-minute segments, four fifteens, six tens, or sixty ones. I don't care how you do it—just do it! By the end of a week you'll have finished an average book and by the end of a year, you'll have finished fifty-two. How quickly can you become a subject matter expert that way? You'll never know until you dig in and read.

- **But Pat, I don't know where to begin!** I've heard that one before. Maybe you closed your last book the day you got your diploma and haven't opened one since. I understand how it is—reading can be intimidating if we think of it as being back in school again. But look at it this way, my friends: this time *you* are in charge of the lesson plan. You can write your own curriculum, as it were. You can read at your own pace. And— this is critical—you can read what interests *you*! In fact, I would go so far as to say that if it doesn't interest you—don't read it. Stay in your field of curiosity. Read books you agree with or books that teach you more about your business or books that expand your worldview. Even though they're not my personal favorites, you can even read novels if they help you relax and think a little more about this amazing world in which we live. Meet me this far: take my challenge for one year and then, if you don't agree that books can change your life you can go back to the remote control. Are you in? If you honestly take me up on this reading challenge, somehow I think I know who will win.

- **Learn how to learn by becoming a reader.** As Lincoln notes, general reading is good for making you an interesting person, but I believe the most effective leaders are those who are in-depth readers. Whatever your field of expertise, become known as the "go-to" person everyone seeks out by drinking deeply of books on that topic. As I said, I make it my aim to finish at least one book a day, and I don't mean just the ones I am writing. But while we're on that topic, becoming an expert in your field through reading also gives you the authority to become—an author. Why not consider writing your own book and becoming a nugget in someone else's roomful of treasure? Writing books is another way to learn how to learn. I once heard David McCullough—author of splendid biographies of Harry Truman, John Adams, and more—say that he did not write a book because he knew a lot about the subject. He wrote the book because he did not know a lot about the subject, but wanted to learn more. "Every book is a new journey," McCullough said "I never felt I was an expert on a subject as I embarked on a project."

Lincoln Lessons for Today
Wisdom to Apply Right Now

1. **Be a reader!** If you're not one already, start today. Jim Rohn, a master of motivation, tells us, "The only thing worse than not reading a book in the last ninety days is not reading a book in the last ninety days and thinking that it doesn't matter."

2. **Make yourself in demand!** Become an expert in the field of your choice through deliberate, in-depth reading.

3. **Take my reading challenge**—I'm sure Lincoln would have issued it first if he'd thought of it. Determine to read—from a book—for one hour (minimum) every day.

CHAPTER 9:

WHAT TO DO WHEN THINGS DON'T WORK OUT

Lincoln's Logs, by Gene Griessman

We live in a things-don't-work-out world. So whenever that happens, we must learn to draw true lessons from the experience.

Just think about all the things that haven't worked out in your life: plans that failed; jobs you didn't get; love that disappointed; opportunities that vanished.

That is the nature of the human experience; it certainly has been the nature of my experience.

Many of my plans failed.

I went into partnership with William F. Berry in New Salem, Illinois where we ran a general store. What happened? We plunged deeper and deeper into debt until finally the store winked out.

I got a job as postmaster, but that paid very little, not enough to support me and pay off my debts, so I tried my hand at surveying, which I did for a short time.

Eventually my debts caught up with me, and at auction, the sheriff sold off my horse, bridle, and surveying instruments. To make matters worse, William Berry died, and I was left with the entire debt—about $1100, which was a staggering sum for me at the time. It took years to pay it off. I called it the National Debt. So, if you say that you've had plans that failed, so have I. Lots of 'em.

So you didn't get a job you really wanted, I know how that feels. When I was twenty-nine years old I was defeated for Speaker of the Illinois State Legislature. I failed in my first quest to go to Congress. But three years later I was elected to the U.S. House of Representatives, for one term. I remained in Washington for a short time, hoping for an attractive position, but nothing that I was interested in was offered.

To a young man struggling with school:
"Must" is the word. I know not how to aid you, save in the assurance of one of mature age, and much severe experience, that you can not fail, if you resolutely determine, that you will not.

– A . L I N C O L N

I returned to Illinois something of a disgrace. While in Congress I had opposed the Mexican War, and now my political enemies had begun to refer to me as the Benedict Arnold of Illinois.

I retired from politics and focused on my law practice. But in the 1850s, I returned to political battle over the slavery issue, and subsequently ran against Stephen Douglas for the U.S. Senate. That didn't work out either. So I certainly know how painful it is to have plans fail and opportunities disappear.

I've mentioned elsewhere that as a young man, I fell in love with Ann Rutledge in New Salem. But she died of a fever, and that broke my heart. Not too long afterward, I was rejected by Mary Owens, a fine young woman from Kentucky. And I was rejected by pretty Sarah Rickard, and I was rejected by Matilda Edwards. Matilda was eighteen years old at the time, and she too was strikingly beautiful. She turned me down flat. As you can well imagine, none of those experiences made me feel very good about myself. I felt humiliated. The rejections hurt beyond words.

So it is inevitable that things won't always work out in your life. What is not inevitable is learning something from them. That is optional.

If you are not careful, however, you may draw an incorrect conclusion from your failure. You may reach a conclusion from your failure that is false, untrue. If you learn a lesson, make sure it is a true one.

Sometimes it is relatively easy to learn a true lesson. You may have said something in anger that you regret. What is the true lesson? Manage your anger. Learn self-control.

You may have entered into a transaction that cost you dearly, because you decided in haste. What is the true lesson? Avoid making hasty, ill-considered decisions. Do due diligence.

You may have failed at a job because you did not have the knowledge required for the job. The true lesson? Acquire the necessary knowledge, and when you have done that, try again.

You may have failed at a job because it is not suited to your temperament. The true lesson? Find another vocation, one that does suit your temperament, for if you do not, you could work hard but never be very good at what you do, nor will you be happy. The true lesson? Rest not until you have found your true work.

I learned that lesson running the store that winked out. I really should say that the store ran me. I was not acquisitive enough; I didn't pay sufficient attention to details—each necessary to be successful in a small business. Learning that lesson cost me money, time, and reputation.

Always look for the true lesson—that small kernel of truth hiding amidst failure's chaff.

I have found that when one is embarrassed, usually the shortest way to get through with it is to quit talking about it or thinking about it, and go at something else.

— A. LINCOLN

The true lesson may be to abandon what you failed at, and never try it again. If that is the true lesson, take it to heart. There's no need to take a whipping twice for the same mistake.

The true lesson may be to try again—but do it differently, or do it in a different place, or at a different time.

Those 1858 debates that I spoke of with Stephen Douglas for the U.S. Senate became famous, and gave me a national reputation.

Senator Douglas and I differed on the burning issue of the spread of slavery. He felt it was all right if slavery spread into the new states that were being formed in the West—if the people of a particular state voted for slavery. He called that concept "popular sovereignty."

In my mind, popular sovereignty was wrong. The ones who had the most to gain or lose were the slaves, and they would not be allowed to vote, so voting slavery up or down was a sham. Slavery should have been put on the road to extinction, not allowed to spread.

I held the view that the nation could not continue half-slave, half-free. My view challenged the very essence of the American experiment. Washington and Jefferson and Adams and the other founding fathers had created a union based on the idea that a permanent union of slave states and free states was possible.

I made my idea public in a speech that I delivered in Springfield, Illinois. That speech is now called the House Divided speech, because in it I stated: "If we could first know where we are, and whither we are tending, we could then better judge what to do, and how to do it. 'A house divided against itself cannot stand.' I believe this government cannot endure, permanently half slave and half free. I do not expect the Union to be dissolved—I do not expect the house to fall—but I do expect it will cease to be divided. It will become all one thing, or all the other… "

After I finished the speech, my closest friends were dismayed. "That'll cost you the election," they told me in no uncertain terms.

And they were right. Douglas pounced on my speech like a tiger. He portrayed me as a dangerous radical. True to my friends' prediction, I did not get to go the U.S. Senate.

What did I learn from the experience? It was not that I was wrong. I was right. It was not that I should keep quiet about that idea. No. A thousand times No.

The true lesson was that the time was not yet ripe for the idea.

Believing in certain great principles of government,
[Lincoln] did not complain because they were unacceptable
to the people, having faith in their ultimate triumph.

– DAVID DAVIS,
U.S. SUPREME COURT JUSTICE AND FRIEND OF LINCOLN

I told my friends: "Gentlemen, you may think that speech was a mistake, but I never have believed it was, and you will see the day when you will consider it was the wisest thing I ever said."

What does my experience say to you? I hope it tells you that sometimes when you fail, you must try again—another way or at another time.

If you learn a true lesson from things that don't work out, you get wisdom. But if you don't, all you get for your trouble is pain.

Living Lincoln: What to Do When Things Don't Work Out
by Pat Williams

I love the brevity of Lincoln's thoughts on this key topic. It tells me that what he really wants us to understand is this: get over it, the quicker the better. As we say in the big leagues, walk it off.

My daughters Sarah and Andrea have provided us with three beautiful little granddaughters, and like most children, when they have an accident, a little "boo-boo," they act as if they've been injured for life—screaming and crying as if a mortal wound has been inflicted. After the tears have dried, if there's any more whimpering their mothers have come up with a wonderful line: "Shake it off!" That's what we hear. "Shake it off, Laila!" "Shake it off, Ava!" "Shake it off, Audri!" There's a wonderful lesson in this for us all—whether we lose a ballgame or fail to make a big sale, whenever we have a setback, it's good counsel: shake it off.

Failure happens, and it's really not such a bad thing when it does. Does that news shock you? Well, here's what one of my personal heroes, Walt Disney, had to say about this topic: "It is good to have a failure when you're young, because it teaches you so much. For one thing, it makes you aware that such a thing can happen to anybody, and once you've lived through the worst, you're never quite as vulnerable afterward." Anybody who's read about Walt's immensely successful life knows he dealt with plenty of failures along the road to the Magic Kingdom.

Failure teaches us what not to do. Without it, how would we know? Seriously. If you never lost a job you wanted or had a deal fall through, how would you know how to do things better the next time?

I've been in the National Basketball Association for forty years. In that time, twenty-three of my teams have gone to the playoffs, five made the finals, and our 1983 76ers squad won the NBA title. Even with all that success, I still tend to ruminate over failures. I'm still working to overcome that tendency.

In 1970, in my first college draft with the Chicago Bulls, on the first round we took a guard named Jimmy Collins from New Mexico State. It turned out he never did anything in the NBA. In that same draft, we passed on two little guards—Calvin Murphy and Nate Archibald. Do you know where those two are today? They are enshrined in Basketball Hall of Fame in Springfield, Massachusetts!

Then in 1984, when I was general manager of the Philadelphia 76ers, we had two first-round picks. We nailed the first one with Charles Barkley. With our second selection, we took Leon Wood from California State University, Fullerton. As it happened, Leon never played much in the NBA. He is now a successful referee in the league, but I still get headaches knowing we passed up John Stockton, arguably the greatest point guard of all time.

The point is, no matter how hard you scout or try to predict the future capability of human beings in any field, you're never going to get it 100% right. But if you keep working at it—learning from your mistakes and making the best judgments you can—in the long run you'll come out ahead.

We've got to know that mistakes are going to happen! For all our hoping and praying and wishing and thinking and odds-analysis—there will still be times when things don't work out. To think otherwise is to set yourself up for the greatest failure of all—the failure to see it coming and to be honest with yourself about your humanness.

I love Lincoln's advice about what to do in the face of failure—to get the right lesson from it, the "true" lesson. People like Walt Disney got that true lesson—the one that said, "Don't give up! Try again! Use a different approach! You can do this!" If he hadn't, just think of where we would be today with no Disneyland or Walt Disney World—maybe even no Mickey Mouse! Can you imagine that? But Walt persevered. When failure knocked him down—and it did often in those early days—he got right up, dusted off his pants, and kept right on walking. That's what to do when things don't work out.

Lincoln Lessons for Today
Wisdom to Apply Right Now

1. **Learn self-control.** Have you ever said something in anger that you now regret? Learn from it! Next time, manage your anger.

2. **Realize that haste really does make waste.** Have you suffered a huge loss as a result of a decision made too quickly? Learn from it! In the future, perform due diligence before making any life-changing decisions.

3. **Gain new skills where needed.** Were you fired from a job you didn't really know how to do? Learn from it! Do what it takes to acquire the necessary knowledge and try again.

4. **Follow your heart.** Have you failed at a job because it really wasn't the right job for you? Learn from it! Discover where your true passions lie and find a way to work in that field.

5. **Stand up for what you really believe in.** Have you lost an argument you truly believed in? Learn from it! Work on your communication skills so that next time the opportunity presents itself, you will be ready. If your idea is a correct one, fight for it. It may simply be ahead of its time.

CHAPTER 10:

IMPROVE YOURSELF

....

Lincoln's Logs, by Gene Griessman

Allow your disappointments to spur you on in your search for personal improvement.

Every day of your life, look for something to improve—beginning with yourself.

Acquire a new skill. Break a bad habit. Begin a good one. Learn a new vocabulary word. Strengthen your will power. Gain more control over your petty feelings and resentments.

This process has been called the power of incrementalism—growing better steadily, unobtrusively, patiently with a great many little steps. People rarely if ever become great at a single bound. Longfellow puts it this way, "The heights by great men, reached and kept, were not attained by sudden flight. But they while their companions slept, were toiling upward in the night."

I learned to benefit from criticism. Any person who listens to no voice but his own is always at risk. My cabinet, as I already mentioned, was composed of outspoken individuals who forcefully, and often, dogmatically expressed their differing views. There is no doubt that their criticism made me better.

When you receive criticism, look at the criticism as potentially valuable information. Analyze the criticism to see what core elements of information it contains.

Sometimes a criticism is like a volcanic eruption. The mixture may contain several basic complaints, some important, some trivial. Ask yourself, "What is in this complaint that I can use?"

Evaluate the critic. Does the person really know? Obviously, all critics are not created equal.

Improve Yourself by Admitting Mistakes

To General Grant, after his stunning victory at Vicksburg

- My dear General: ...When you got below and took Port Gibson, Grand Gulf and vicinity, I thought you should go down the river and join General Banks; and when you turned northward, east of the Big Black, I feared it was a mistake. I now wish to make the personal acknowledgement that you were right and I was wrong. Yours very truly...

– A. Lincoln

Be willing to change your behavior, your habits, your ideas in the presence of new information. My contemporary Ralph Waldo Emerson put it this way: "A foolish consistency is the hobgoblin of little minds, adored by little statesmen and philosophers and divines. With consistency a great soul has simply nothing to do. He may as well concern himself with the shadow on the wall."

For many years Horace Greeley, the editor of the New York *Tribune*, was American's single most influential journalist. He was one of my earliest supporters, but he also was one of my severest critics.

In the end, Mr. Greeley paid me one of the finest compliments that I ever received. Here's what he said: "Lincoln gladly profited by the teachings of events and circumstances, no matter how adverse or unwelcome.... There was probably no year of his life that he was not a wiser, cooler, better man than he had been the year preceding."

Some compliments I certainly don't deserve, but I do think, with no false modesty, that my entire life was devoted to self-improvement. One reason I had so much success at self-improvement, was because I had so much to improve. I could start on almost anything.

Have you ever heard about Benjamin Franklin's plan for self-improvement? He wrote about it in his autobiography. When Benjamin Franklin was a young man, he wrote down thirteen virtues—moderation, frugality, industry—thirteen of 'em, that he wanted in his life. Those virtues became guidelines for his career.

Like Franklin, look for something that you can improve every day, beginning with yourself—but do not stop there. Franklin didn't. Look for some way to make your world better.

Plant a flower, support a worthy cause, right a wrong, conduct a scientific experiment, make your company run more efficiently, compose a song, cure a disease, start a philanthropy, teach a child to read.

For as long as I can remember, I wanted it to be said of me that the world was a better place because I had lived in it.

A poet defined success this way: "To leave the world a bit better, whether by a healthy child, a garden plot, a redeemed social condition. To know that even one soul has breathed easier because you have lived... this is to have succeeded." I say it's a great way to make up for those times when things don't work out.

A capacity, and taste, for reading gives access to whatever has already been discovered by others. It is the key, or one of the keys, to the already solved problems. And not only so. It gives a relish, and facility, for successfully pursuing the unsolved ones.

– A . L I N C O L N

Living Lincoln: Improve Yourself
By Pat Williams

People who know me will tell you I'm a stickler for making every day better than the one that came before it. They won't get an argument from me.

I firmly believe that we are all works in progress, and that the best is yet to come. Here are a few things I do to make sure my today is better than my yesterday:

1. **I start out everyday by spending a few minutes with my personal Commander in Chief,** the God who gave me life and who renews it daily. I pray for my family, my friends, my co-workers, and for wisdom regarding my decisions that day.

2. **I exercise my body.** You've undoubtedly heard the expression "use it or lose it," and I am here to tell you that with every passing year the meaning of that phrase takes on new color. If we stop moving, we will in time literally lose our ability to move! I don't know about you, but I am just fine with putting off rigor mortis for as long as possible. My daily routine involves running—always— and then working out on any machine I can find. Since

I travel frequently, I can't always depend on having the same equipment available everywhere I go, but I manage to find something—a stationary cycle, a treadmill, a rowing machine. You and I *can* always find some way to keep the body moving on a regular daily basis. I recommend it.

3. **I exercise my mind.** It's rare to see me without a book in my hands. Over the years, I've learned to take one with me wherever I go. I go into this more in Chapter 8, but I can't stress the message enough—what you get from a book will last you far longer than any momentary diversion. There is also evidence that reading staves off Alzheimer's disease—and I think we'd all like to keep that enemy at bay.

4. **I eat right.** It really does matter! We can get away with the Big Macs and fries for a few years, but if you ask me, why bother? Ultimately, fast food just brings you down and the longer you indulge in it, the harder it is to break away. I'm grateful my parents pointed me toward a life of health from the beginning and that I've never been tempted to indulge in destructive habits like smoking or drinking. But even if you've been stuffing your body with junk all your life, the good news is you can turn that around with your very next meal. I'm not trying to preach here—I just want to see you live longer and better. And I believe the pathway to that better life is only found with proper nutrition. Think about this: everything we need for life is available to us without any cans, bags, or boxes. And those foods—the whole foods—are far better for you in the end.

5. **I call people.** OK, I admit this is one area where I've been slow to make it into the 21st century—I almost never use e-mail. Why wear out my fingers on a keyboard when

dialing a number is so much faster? And on the phone, there is much less chance of any misunderstanding occurring. Besides, I like people! I enjoy "collecting people," as I call it, and while e-mail has done amazing things by helping us keep in touch with one another, there is just no substitute in my mind for a good old-fashioned conversation. I once heard that when Donald Trump arrives in his office, he picks up his phone and begins calling people. He talks to people all morning long. Then after lunch, he moves on to the next round.

I appreciate Lincoln's thoughts about leaving the world a better place and leaving it better because you were here. What a dynamic idea that is! Think about all the people who've come and gone. How many of them invested their lives in improving the world?

Far too many of us waste time trying to figure out why we are here and never get around to actually doing something with the precious gift of life we've been given. As much as it is up to you, let it one day be said that you served your generation and made life better for the next.

Lincoln Lessons for Today

Wisdom to Apply Right Now

1. **Look for something to improve every day!** Maybe it's how you dress—I know it sounds shallow, but people do have to look at you, after all. Or maybe you can add a new word to your vocabulary every day. Nothing improves your chances for success more than your command of the language.

2. **Take baby steps.** Keep in mind that improvement need not be radical—the best way to improve is slowly, incrementally, one step, one day, at a time.

3. **Don't stop at *self*-improvement**—look for ways to better your world. Let it be said of you that you left the world a better place than the one you entered.

4. **Believe in yourself!** Lincoln said, "The way for a young man to rise is to improve himself every way he can, never suspecting that anybody wishes to hinder him."

CHAPTER 11:

THE IMPORTANCE OF DIVERSITY

....

Lincoln's Logs, by Gene Griessman

I f you ever meet someone who thinks exactly the same way that you do about everything, one of you is unnecessary.

I began to learn to value diversity in the little settlements of the frontier where I grew up. We understood its importance. Oh, we didn't call it that, but we understood the concept.

We welcomed people if they knew something that we didn't; if they could do something that we couldn't. One person could shoe horses, another could make shoes; one person could grow corn, another could mill it; one person could make bricks, another could lay them; one person could weave cloth, another could tailor it. Do you see where I'm going? One person could teach. Another could learn.

We accepted one another because we needed one another. Our differences made us useful to one another, held us together and enabled us to live a better life. Ours was an organic solidarity, not a mechanical or an artificial one. There was a unity in those little settlements that was based on differences, on reciprocity, not homogeneity.

I took that same philosophy with me to the White House.

When I became President, I had never had a single day of executive experience. I had never managed anything larger than our little, two-man law firm in Springfield, Illinois. Suddenly I was thrust into the role of chief executive officer of the United States of America. We often called the

President the "chief magistrate" in the 1800s. It was a daunting challenge. By the closing years of the war, there were one million men in uniform. Just imagine running an organization with a million people in it, and that was just the military.

Is that a scary thought? It was scary to a lot of people.

But I knew something that many of them did not understand. I knew that I did not have to know everything; that I could surround myself with people who knew more than I did, who could do what I couldn't do.

My cabinet was probably the most diverse cabinet ever assembled in Washington. I chose people who had skills that I lacked, knowledge that I did not possess. Three members of my cabinet had run against me for President and felt they should have won. They knew that they were better qualified than I, and they probably were right.

[Lincoln] is the first man I have talked with in the United States who in no single instance reminded me of the difference between himself and myself, of the difference of color.

— FREDERICK DOUGLASS,
FORMER SLAVE, ABOLITIONIST, AND ORATOR

My Secretary of State was William Seward. He had been Governor of the state of New York. He was a college graduate, a brilliant man, a prominent senator, and my biggest rival for the nomination.

My Secretary of Treasury was Salmon Chase, who knew a great deal about finance, and had been Governor of Ohio. The others were just as talented and opinionated. They gossiped about one another, ridiculed one another and me.

Managing such a group was not easy, but together we possessed great knowledge and formidable skills. I kept these proud and talented people on the team as long as they made a contribution, even some who were not loyal to me. However I felt I could not deprive the county of their talents just because of my personal dislike for them.

There's an important success principle here:

You can do whatever you need to do, go as far as you want to go, if you can manage people who know more than you do and can do what you can't.

The easy, comfortable approach is to work with and enjoy people who think pretty much the same as you do. And there's nothing wrong with that, if you do not limit yourself to that approach. After all, there's an old saying: "Birds of a feather flock together." For your closest friends, it's comfortable not to be arguing all the time about basic assumptions. It's a pleasant experience to be with people who see the world the way you do.

If you want to grow and improve yourself and any organization that you lead, make some friends and find some associates who are different from you, who have had different experiences from yours, who see the world in a different way. They will help you discover solutions to problems that you cannot solve, and see opportunities that you might otherwise miss.

This is the story of Lincoln's political genius revealed
through his extraordinary array of personal qualities
that enabled him to form friendships with men who had
previously opposed him; to repair injured feelings that, left
untended, might have escalated into permanent hostility;
to assume responsibility for the failures of subordinates;
to share credit with ease, and to learn from mistakes.

– DORIS KEARNS GOODWIN,
TEAM OF RIVALS: THE POLITICAL GENIUS OF ABRAHAM LINCOLN.
NEW YORK: SIMON & SCHUSTER, 2005, INTRODUCTION

The Almighty must love diversity. That's why he makes so much of it. Diversity is as natural as the trillion shapes and shades of the flowers of spring or the leaves of autumn. What is unnatural is sameness—it's uninteresting and limiting. Diversity brings new solutions to our ever-changing environment.

We should treat those who are different from us with tolerance, not just because it is the right thing to do, but because we need them. If you want to rise to new and higher levels, you will value and use diversity.

I hope there will be no persecution, no bloody work after the
war is over. None need expect me to take part in hanging
or killing them. Enough lives have been sacrificed. We must
extinguish our resentment if we expect harmony and union.

– A. LINCOLN
TO HIS CABINET, JUST HOURS BEFORE HIS ASSASSINATION

Living Lincoln:
The Importance of Diversity
by Pat Williams

I've always been fascinated with putting sports teams together, but I have discovered that the same principles of great athletics teams transfers totally to teams in business, education, churches, science, and the military. The principles are universal. My long experience in sports and my study of the topic has convinced me that effective teams both understand and apply the eight timeless qualities that must be in place. Let me share these principles with you briefly.

1. **Talent:** To have a great team you must have outstanding talent. You can't be afraid of talent, even though talented people are often creative, imaginative, and independent in their thinking. Without gifted team members, you're always going to be limited.

2. **Outstanding leadership:** There's never been a great team that didn't have a great leader. Everything rises and falls on leadership. It always has and it always will.

3. **Commitment:** Terrific teams have made a total commitment. You ask me, "Committed to what?" 1) Committed to each other; 2) committed to excellence; 3) committed to competing in a highly competitive marketplace; and 4) committed to winning!

4. **Passion:** I've learned that great teams are passionate about what they do. They go about every aspect of their day with energy, enthusiasm, excitement—it radiates through an organization.

5. **T.E.A.M.S.:** Together Everybody Achieves More Successfully. I love watching the Clydesdale horses on TV commercials at Christmastime. Did you know that one Clydesdale can pull a load of 5,000 pounds? Two of them together can pull between 15,000 and 20,000 pounds, and four can pull up to 50,000 pounds. It's amazing what we can do when we pull together.

6. **Empowerment:** On successful teams people are rooting for each other, they're encouraging each other, cheering for one another, uplifting, helping out teammates when they're struggling, rooting for their success.

7. **Respect:** R-E-S-P-E-C-T is more than just a great song by Aretha Franklin. Great teams are built on respect, which leads to trust, which leads to loyalty, which leads to love, which leads to friendship.

8. **Character counts:** Great teams are made up of men and women of character—old-fashioned stuff like honesty, integrity, personal responsibility, work ethic, perseverance, and courage. Character never goes out of fashion.

Try building those eight principles into your team, and watch what happens.

By the way, I've been practicing this whole team-building exercise in my home for years. We have built a family of great diversity with nineteen children—fourteen of whom have been adopted from four foreign countries—South Korea, the Philippines, Romania, and Brazil. It's truly a United Nations family. By now seven grandchildren have arrived and we've got another generation of diversity coming along. Whenever we take the grandkids out for Sunday lunch, it truly looks like a UN Security Council meeting.

Our world is becoming more and more diverse—just look around you! It's important that we embrace it.

Lincoln Lessons for Today
Wisdom to Apply Right Now

1. **We need to realize our interdependency.** Lincoln said that in the settlements of the frontier, people accepted one another because they needed one another. That fact has not changed. We think we are more independent, but it's not true. We need each other more in our global economy than ever before.

2. **You do not need to know everything!** Surround yourself with a diverse team you can learn from. Lincoln was not afraid of having men who disagreed with him on his cabinet. He believed those divergent perspectives strengthened the team. It does!

3. **See life through other people's eyes.** Seek out relationships with associates who think differently from the way you view things. Seeing life from various worldviews expands our thinking and enhances leadership ability. Just consider what America could be like if Republicans and Democrats really *tried* to see the issues through each other's eyes?

4. **Be willing to accept people from all cultural backgrounds.** As a result of adopting fourteen children from four different countries (added to my four birth-children, plus one more from a second marriage), I've learned that the world is indeed a small place—and it's getting smaller. (At least it sure feels that way at my house!) We must reach out to people of different nationalities, different faiths, and different heritage. We all have to get along here on planet Earth, so let it start with you and me.

CHAPTER 12:

THE BEST WAY TO AVOID FAILURES

....

Lincoln's Logs, by Gene Griessman

The best way to avoid failures is—don't attempt anything. That way you never fail…because you never try.

"He who aims at nothing shall surely hit it," is the way I heard an old pioneer in Indiana put it.

Every success formula I ever saw had the possibility of failure built in. Generally, the greater the opportunity, the greater the risk of failing.

Have you ever noticed that somebody who's never been sick a day in his life, when he finally does get sick, just goes in a hurry—just like that? But somebody who's been sickly all his life and just hangs on forever seems to build up immunity to *everything*.

I built up immunity to failure by failing so many times. I probably developed failure antibodies. One reason I was able to get through the early disasters of the War was my previous experience with failure.

You probably could achieve even greater success than you have known, if you were not held back by an inordinate fear of failure. Could it be that you are too risk-averse?

I learned that there is life after failure. When you fall down, you look to see what you stumbled over, and you pick yourself up. You move on. You don't whine. You don't blame somebody else. I find quite as much material for a lecture in those points wherein I have failed, as in those wherein I have been moderately successful.

When you're embarrassed, usually the shortest way to get through with it is to quit talking about it and thinking about it, and go at something else. In fact, you might want to use a four-letter word, beginning with the letter "n": N-E-X-T.

Every day, you're either dying a little, or being reborn. I tried to keep on growing, living, learning, being reborn every day.

Not long ago, I saw a poster with a list of my failures printed beneath my picture. I told the clerk at the store where the poster was on sale that it was sort of embarrassing to see some of my most conspicuous failures emblazoned on a poster. He told me it was an inspirational poster.

Inspirational! Well, I can tell you this. When you're going through bankruptcy, and experiencing unrequited love, rejection, scorn, political defeats and humiliations—it's not very inspirational! Failure never is inspirational at the time. It may be in retrospect—but if recounting my failures is an inspiration to others, I suppose I don't mind.

Only a few months before I was nominated for President, the Philadelphia *Press* ran a feature article about the upcoming convention that listed forty-five possible candidates. Do you want to know what number I was? My name was not even on the list.

At age forty-nine, I was out of politics, with little hope of returning to high office. My political fortunes were at an all-time low. An editor wrote: "The Hon. Abe Lincoln is undoubtedly the most unfortunate politician that has ever attempted to rise in Illinois. In everything he undertakes, politically, he seems doomed to failure."

When that was written I had seven years left to live.

Yet during those next seven years I did virtually everything I'm remembered for today…after I had been written off.

Your greatest accomplishment may just take place in the next seven years of your life. Everything that you have done thus far may be preparation for your ultimate work, a prelude to the most important contributions of your life.

Living Lincoln: What Failure Means for You
By Pat Williams

I love Lincoln's point about there being life after every failure. He is so right!

After the end of my first marriage, it took awhile for me to have the courage to admit publicly that I had failed in a way that mattered so much to me. But once I began confessing it—not only to my friends but in the spotlight whenever I spoke, it was amazing to see the doors open up as hundreds of men realized they weren't alone. No matter what your biggest failure is—others have fallen there too and would love your company.

Lincoln said he was embarrassed by a public recounting of his failures—but I've learned that the best kind of life to live is a transparent one. People long for honesty and authenticity from their leaders. Nothing connects people faster than the words, "I'm no different than you."

I've also learned there is definitely life after failure. Following that darkest period in my life, the sun did come out again—and her name is Ruth. At this writing we are celebrating more than twelve blessed years together and she is truly my rock.

Reborn every day—what a great thought. I like to think that is true in my life as well. Has it ever occurred to you that each day is like a mini-life? The morning is the birth of the day, the daytime is where we do our walking around and living, and then we go to sleep. So each day that we wake, we're being given another opportunity at life.

Rick Warren, author of *The Purpose-Driven Life*, challenges us to ask ourselves why God would leave us here for even one more minute if he didn't have a purpose for our lives. Lincoln discovered that purpose in his last seven years (a biblical number of completion, by the way). Next time you find yourself out of a job, or feeling lost and scared after a huge failure in your life, remember Abraham Lincoln. Your best years just could be ahead of you!

Lincoln Lessons for Today
Wisdom to Apply Right Now

1. **Don't let fear hold you back!** Risk-taking is an essential element of success. Next time the fear of failure threatens to grip you, think about Lincoln and his immunity to failure—built up by failing so often. In order to lead like Lincoln, you may have to learn to fail like Lincoln too.

2. **Realize that there is life after failure.** If you fall, pick yourself back up and see what you have left. Then, as the saying goes, *try, try again.*

3. **Never write yourself off!** If anyone accuses you of being doomed to fail, think of the editor who once wrote off Abraham Lincoln—a man whose greatest success, and the highest office in the land, lay ahead of him.

CHAPTER 13:

HOW TO DESTROY AN ENEMY

....

Lincoln's Logs, by Gene Griessman

During the war, inventors often came to Washington to demonstrate ingenious ways to destroy the enemy—repeating pistols, rifles, mines, balloons, submarines, ironclads. Some of them worked so well that they helped turn the course of the war.

But I never forgot that the best way to destroy an enemy—the very best way—is to turn an enemy into a friend. That strategy has been employed so seldom that you would think it is a secret weapon. Perhaps it is.

Avoid turning arguments into quarrels. There's a big difference. A quarrel is an argument that's been infected with negative, personal feelings. Have you ever been arguing with someone, and after a while sensed it change from an argument into a quarrel? You could actually *feel* it happening inside you. Whenever that happens, stop. The very best time to stop a quarrel is before it begins.

A wise man once said: "There is nothing so pathetic as a person who is determined to be crucified on the cross of a personal grievance." All the time and energy you spend getting even could be devoted to getting ahead.

Avoid turning an opponent into an enemy. An opponent may disagree with you on a particular subject, but still like you. An enemy may agree with you on a particular subject, but dislike you so much that he or she will oppose everything you do.

This doesn't mean that you should never disagree. If you show me someone who never disagrees with anybody about anything, I will show you someone who will never leave a mark on the world. That person will come and go without notice.

I argued all the time. I'm a lawyer. Lawyers get paid to argue.

To every one he was pleasant and cordial. Yet they all felt it was his word that went at last; that every case was open until he gave his decision. This impression of authority, or reserve force, Mr. Lincoln always gave to those around him.

— CHARLES DANA,
ASSISTANT SECRETARY OF WAR UNDER LINCOLN

But I learned to argue in such a way that I could still be friends with the person I was arguing with. I learned to disagree without being disagreeable, to contend without being contentious.

Don't think that this came easily to me. I have a temper, and when I was a young man, I would call those who opposed me thieves, and liars, and knaves. More than once I got into fist-fights.

I often succeeded in turning my opponents into enemies. I wrote anonymous letters in which I mercilessly attacked those who opposed me. I mocked and ridiculed. I could be cutting and vicious. Once I mimicked an opponent so cruelly that he left the room in tears.

It is scarcely known today, but I once was involved in a duel. We actually met on a little island in the middle of the Mississippi River. His name was James Shields. Our seconds worked out a compromise, and the duel was averted at the very last moment.

That experience taught me an important lesson—that quarreling does not pay. Quarreling has consequences, and those consequences can be costly. Shakespeare advised: "Beware of entrance to a quarrel, but being in, bear it that the opposed may beware thee."

That is good advice, but not the best: Quarrel not at all.

No one who has resolved to make the most of himself can spare time for personal contention. Better to yield the right of way to a dog than to be bitten by him in contesting for the right. Even if you kill the dog, you will not cure the bite.

Life is too short to spend it in quarrels, brooding over slights. By the time I got to the White House, I could honestly say that if I did get up a temper, I did not have sufficient time to keep it up. I was too busy doing something else.

What to do if you do get in a quarrel? If you are in the wrong, admit it. If you were unpleasant, apologize.

Let me tell you an experience I had after the battle of Antietam that taught me volumes about the best way to deal with an enemy. Antietam was the single bloodiest day in American history. More men died that day than died in the Revolutionary War, which lasted over eight years.

After the battle I was asked to come down and visit the wounded. As I walked amongst them, offering a handshake or a word of cheer, I came to a soldier boy who lay on a cot. He was just a boy, no more than fourteen or fifteen. They told me that he was mortally wounded. It was clear he did not have long to live.

I stopped beside him. His uniform was not blue. It was gray. I reached out my hand to him and said, "Would you shake my hand if you knew my name?" He opened his eyes—they were glazed: "Who are you, suh?"

"My name is Lincoln; I'm President of the United States."

There was a long pause. I did not know what he would say or do. I knew that my name was despised by millions. For all I knew, in one final act of defiance, he might spit in my face.

The better part of one's life consists of his friendships.

— A . LINCOLN

He somehow found the strength to lift himself up on the cot, looked round the room, and then at me. "Suh—I reckon I don't see no enemies in this place." Then he extended his arm, took my hand in his, and squeezed it for the longest time.

I cannot tell you how much that meant to me.

The best way to destroy an enemy? Turn your enemy into a friend.

Living Lincoln: Turn Your Enemies into Friends

By Pat Williams

As you have seen with your own eyes, undoubtedly, many times in stadiums, ballparks, sports arenas, or on television—the world of professional sports is a universe of quarrels. The good news, however, is that in most cases we are able to leave the quarrel on the court or the playing field. Would that it were so in other arenas. What a boon this advice could be, for example, in our often-contentious society.

Have you noticed in recent years that the intensity of the rhetoric is ramping up almost daily? Leaders in particular, often some of the most demonized individuals in any organization, need to learn this skill—avoid turning arguments into quarrels.

I was listening recently to some wonderful tape recordings done by Lawrence Ritter for his famous baseball book *The Glory of Their Times*—a marvelous book originally published in 1966. The recordings are of magnificent interviews with old-time ball players that eventually led to Ritter's best-selling book. On one of them, Fred Snodgrass, who played centerfield for the New York Giants in the early part of the twentieth century, was reminiscing about the famous National League playoff game at end of the 1908 season.

The Chicago Cubs came onto Polo Grounds to play the Giants in a one-game match that would determine who would play in the World Series. Frank Chance, who went on to earn the nickname "Peerless Leader," was the Cubs' first baseman. The Giants decided to get him into a fight before the game and get him thrown out. Since Giants' pitcher "Iron Man" Joe McGinnity was not scheduled to pitch that day, he became the designated provoker.

McGinnity confronted Chance and harassed him and generally did everything he could to make Chance explode with anger so he would start a fight and get thrown out of game before it even started. But Chance did not react. He could see clearly what the Giants were up to. Not only did Chance not respond to McGinnity's taunts, but he helped lead the Cubs to victory that day, and then a triumph over the Detroit Tigers in the World Series—the last time in that century that the Cubs won a World Series. It happened over 100 years ago, and that '08 championship may never have happened if Frank Chance had lost his temper.

Speaking of things that have changed in the last hundred years, I think many of you would agree that civility has become sorely lacking in our society—and the tension seems at times to be increasing. Look around. It's not helping! So let me take this opportunity to issue you a challenge:

No matter what your position or with whom you relate on a daily basis, see if you can **go for one whole week without quarreling**—with anyone. Not even the guy you don't like on radio or TV! After that first week, go for a second, and a third, and so on until quarreling is driven from your life.

When my children were younger, I used to challenge them to what I titled The 90-Day Test. Here's how it worked: I'd say, "Kids, for next ninety days, the only words that can leave your lips must be words that are kind, gentle, uplifting, encouraging, and helpful. I expect ninety straight days of this with everybody you meet—including your brothers and sisters. If at anytime during the ninety days you blow it, you've got to go back to Day One and start all over again"—which happened a lot. "But if you can get to end of the ninety days successfully every relationship you have will be dramatically altered. You'll never want to go back to your old behavior or speaking to others in any other way. This is powerful stuff!"

I'm not saying my children, who are now all adults, ever got it mastered—none can reach that lofty goal. But it doesn't mean we shouldn't try every day. It is very gratifying to realize my children have all become, for the most part, polite, courteous, and very careful in how they select the words that leave their lips. Once those words are gone, they're out there forever. You can't get them back.

I encouraged my kids, and I encourage you, to try to see life through others' eyes. Realize that each one of us believes we are right about whatever our strongly held beliefs and opinions might be. And most of us really do want a better workplace, a more successful company, a happier family, and a greater America. We may disagree on how to get there, but as long as we're all moving in the same direction I believe we'll arrive at our chosen destinations. And won't it be so much better to travel with friends?

On a radio show I host in Orlando I recently interviewed an author who was talking about raising children. He talked about how important it is to teach your children to be kind, to be nice! "The world out there is downright mean," he said. "Everyone is trying to see if they can out mean each other." My guest went on to opine that rudeness seems to be the order of the day. The world out there has gotten so mean, so confrontational. We see it on television everyday—just in-your-face meanness, as if it's really cool to be mean. People scream at each other on television all day long, with everyone fighting to get in the last word. On some shows I've seen, they're all talking at the same time. Half the time, I want to paddle them, or send them to their room, or make them take a time out—or make them take the 90-Day Test!

We've *got* to teach our kids how to be nice. They say that kids learn more by what is caught than what is taught—so what better way to start the teaching than through our own example. Be nice to everyone you meet.

Learn to turn your enemies into friends, and teach your kids to do the same.

Lincoln Lessons for Today
Wisdom to Apply Right Now

1. **Destroy your enemies—by turning them into your friends!** Next time you find yourself face-to-face with an enemy, think of the Rebel soldier who shook hands with Abraham Lincoln, on his deathbed.

2. **Avoid turning arguments into quarrels and opponents into enemies.** Keep negative, personal feelings out of the discussion. Getting personal is a surefire way to turn an opponent into an enemy.

3. **Determine not to quarrel at all.** If you feel the emotions rising within you, choose that moment to stop talking. Remember the 90-Day Test.

CHAPTER 14:

WHAT TO DO WHEN YOU DON'T HAVE A ROADMAP

Lincoln's Logs, by Gene Griessman

So—big changes are occurring in your world, in your business, in your personal life? I know what that's like.

I know from personal experience what it feels like to live in a time of great change, when old ways are being abandoned, when it's not clear what they will be replaced with, when you are called on to lead—but you don't have a roadmap.

In the 1860s we knew that we had to move forward, but there was great confusion about which way to go, which path to take. What had begun as a rebellion was turning into a revolution.

The Founding Fathers, prudent and wise as they were, had invented a government and created a Constitution, but they had neglected to tell future generations what to do if a civil war occurred. It fell to my generation, and eventually to me as President, to somehow work out what to do in that time of profound change.

When I was born, one in eight Americans was a slave. Can you imagine that? And in many parts of the country, the slaves far outnumbered the free. North and South extracted profit from that pernicious system, and both were corrupted by it. The cost of ending human bondage was to be paid in blood, rivers of blood.

It was a time of technological change. I saw the beginnings of a communication revolution. In the history of the world, there had been only two major communication revolutions before it. I saw the beginnings of the third, which continues to the present day.

The first revolution was the invention of writing, the second, the invention of the printing press, and the third was the application of electricity to the communication process with the invention of the telegraph.

I spent a lot of time in the telegraph office, learning how to communicate in a new way. Today you have what you call the Internet, so that now you can communicate with people everywhere in the world. Do you know how amazing that ability is? I suppose only someone like myself who once lived without these inventions can fully appreciate what it means. Come to think about it, I lived through a social revolution and saw the beginnings of a communication revolution.

In Mr. Lincoln's administration, the world has seen and wondered at the greatest sign and marvel of our day, to wit, a plain working man of the people, with no more culture, instruction, or education than any such working man may obtain for himself, called on to conduct the passage of a great nation through a crisis involving the destinies of the whole world.

– HARRIET BEECHER STOWE, ABOLITIONIST AND AUTHOR OF *UNCLE TOM'S CABIN*

It is difficult to predict everything that will happen in a revolution, but you gain an advantage if you can predict its general direction.

In the 1850s, as I already mentioned, I could see that the United States could not permanently continue half slave and half free—that a house divided against itself could not stand. I predicted that the nation would become all one or all the other. That insight gave me a political advantage, and helped me become President. I was able to position myself strategically, and wait for events to unfold.

Just because something is new does not make it good or bad. Don't oppose something just because it's new or different. Banish the expression: "We've always done it this way."

There was a time when people did not do everything we do now—from eating with knives, forks, and spoons to voting for our leaders. The changes that may be causing you stress today will someday be explained to a young person as "the way we've always done it here."

A friend of mine, whom I respect greatly, once told me that he would change his mind and his behavior on a dime, in the presence of new information. I like that attitude. It's intellectually honest, and it's strategic and practical, too.

Instead of fighting change, learn how to use it.

I could have insisted on writing by hand all my messages to my generals. In fact, I did do that sometimes. I had worked hard as a boy to acquire the old technology of good penmanship. But I learned to use a new technology—the telegraph.

When change occurs, adopt a flexible attitude. Which reminds me of a story.

A young man applied for a teaching job. The committee asked him if he believed the world was flat or round. He replied, "It doesn't matter to me. I'm prepared to teach it either way."

The moral of that story, if it has one, is if you're in a precarious situation, it sometimes pays to be flexible.

The changes in my day were different in some respects from those in yours, but there are similarities, and lessons can be drawn from them.

If you are a leader during a time of change:

1. **Be willing to invest in yourself.** Acquire the necessary knowledge to use new tools—even if you have to hire a coach or teacher or pay for books and journals out of your own purse. Remember, I did that in Springfield, Illinois in order to prepare for my first patent infringement case. That proved to be a good investment.

2. **Reassure your people.** They will feel awkward and clumsy. They may have acquired a reputation for being skillful with the old technology, and when they are required to change, may lose the esteem of their fellows. They may feel embarrassed and frustrated that they can't do their work as well as they once did. There will be what you call today a learning curve, perhaps a steep learning curve, and you must be prepared to accept it.

3. **Communicate your vision.** Do not assume that the people you lead can see what you see. I freely confess that I did not control events, but as a leader I did have an opportunity to interpret events and help those I led to understand them. Your capacity to reframe questions and situations will determine how effective a leader you become.

4. **Monitor the situation.** Establish lines of communication in order to stay informed. Make it your business to know what's working and what isn't working, so that you can make necessary adjustments. Your goal is to do more of what's working, and quickly abandon or modify what isn't working. "The voyage of the best ship is a zigzag line of a hundred tacks," is the way Ralph Waldo Emerson put it.

5. **Appeal to the better angels of people's nature.** Bring out the best in them. Initially they will think about what they have to give up. That's human nature. You must emphasize

in a believable manner what are the benefits. Help them understand that a time of change is an opportunity to learn new skills, make new friends, break out of old prisons.

6. **Remain optimistic.** Even if you have inward doubts, try to convey optimism. That reminds me of an old farmer who told me, "When you borrow, try to borrow from a pessimist. He won't expect to get it back."

Finding great opportunities in times of change depends on your ability to see. Seeing is not easy. A writer by the name of Walter Lippman once wrote, "What we see depends on where we stand, and the habits of our eyes." That's a profound idea.

---

*If we could first know where we are, and whither we are tending, we could then better judge **what** to do, and **how** to do it.*

— A. LINCOLN

What we see does indeed depend on where we stand. We may stand at such a low elevation that we may not be able to see our final destination on a distant mountain peak. It may be obscured by undergrowth or low hills before us. We will need to climb to a higher place to clearly see the goal in the distance.

During the War, I had a number of generals who were good at tactics, which is a valuable skill. They knew how to achieve short-term objectives, win skirmishes or even battles. But they could not see the bigger picture. They were too close to the ground, too close to their troops.

General McClellan was that kind of general. He was a genius at turning raw recruits into disciplined soldiers. He was very effective at raising morale.

But he was totally lost when it came to seeing the larger picture. In fact, he wasn't all that good at winning single battles, either.

General Meade was a fine tactical general. He was responsible for repulsing General Lee's army at Gettysburg, but he was not a good strategic general. It was not until I found General Grant that I had a general who could see beyond winning the battle to winning the war.

What you see depends on where you stand, but it also depends on the habits of your eyes. People who are conventional look at things in conventional ways, which is to say, the way most everybody else has always seen them. Conventional people do not come up with innovations because they cannot grasp that there is any way but the old way of thinking about something. New ways of thinking come from individuals who often don't know the right way to do something, so they come up with a way of their own.

John Ruskin wrote: "The greatest thing a human being does on this earth is to see something and tell what he saw in plain language. Hundreds can talk for one who can think, but thousands can think for one who can see. To see clearly and speak plainly is poetry, prophecy, and religion all in one."

What to do when you are called upon to lead in a time of change, when you don't have a roadmap? Teach yourself to see clearly and speak plainly.

Living Lincoln: What to Do When You Don't Have a Roadmap
By Pat Williams

Great changes are happening in our time. Maybe they are happening in your business or in your world. Hardly a day goes by without major change occurring somewhere. It may be planned change, accidentally discovered change, or change we cannot stop—like a hurricane, or a divorce. But change is the one constant we can depend on in life.

Lincoln identifies himself as a man intimately familiar with dynamic, painful change. What do you do when old ways are abandoned and the new ways are not yet clear—when you are called upon to lead without a roadmap?

In my own career, it was back in the mid-1980s that I began to see the general direction of expansion in the world of professional sports. So I went looking for cities likely to welcome a new NBA team. This ability—one I'd carefully honed, by the way—to read the pulse of the moment led to the eventual birth of the Orlando Magic basketball team.

There are techniques I've learned about reading that pulse that I believe will serve you well, no matter what the business climate or era. It's an ability that requires 1) **constantly reading and staying on top of all the latest news in my field**—in my case, sports. I read five newspapers every day and every sports magazine as soon as it's out—and I've done that since I was twelve years old. Another is 2) **staying in close touch with people in the industry.** I live on the telephone, checking with my cohorts in business and working very closely with the media. I have found that it's important to befriend writers and sportscasters, because they are a fountain of knowledge and information—and I've discovered they're often willing to share it confidentially. Knowledge is power. If you are knowledgeable about what is going on in your industry, you can be a real force throughout your career. And then 3) **listen to your fans.** Pay attention to your customers. They are often loaded with great ideas, so if they're willing to share them, pay attention. These people may be your best source of new ideas and techniques—ideas that may be more effective than what you're currently doing. Be open, receptive, and available to your public. Never cut yourself off from your power base. And always, always be courteous.

What else can help you position yourself for future growth? Why not take that advice Lincoln has given you as a leader and apply it to your personal professional growth:

1. **Be willing to invest in yourself.** Attend seminars, take classes, and learn, learn, learn. Remember that one of the best ways to learn is by reading a book!

2. **Reassure yourself.** You may feel uncertain about a new direction your company or your life is taking. But you've been in circumstances like this before. You survived it then and you'll get through it now. If there's something you need to learn in order to adapt to this new direction—learn it. Go easy on yourself and don't expect to change overnight. Accept your own learning curve.

3. **Communicate your vision—to yourself!** One reason I believe many leaders fail in the implementation of new vision is that in addition to poorly communicating that vision to the people they lead—they are unclear themselves about that vision. Make sure that you have a clear picture of where you're likely headed before you move ahead— especially before you try to recruit people to ride on your bus.

4. **Monitor the situation.** Take a daily assessment of your own personal progress. Some people use prayer, some use journaling, others like to check off lists in their Franklin Planners, or even process their thoughts through a blog. However you do it, make sure you keep an eye on your progress toward your life goals. If what you are doing is

working—keep it up. If not, look for another battle strategy.

5. **Appeal to the better angels of people's nature.** Determine to work with yourself and others in a way that brings out the best in everyone concerned in your project. The ultimate benefits will be greater peace and civility in the workplace—and very likely greater success for your business. A time of change is always, always, always an opportunity for something new and amazing to happen.

6. **Remain optimistic.** Optimism, in my view, has always been one of the keys to great leadership. It's critical you remain positive and upbeat, no matter what the truth of the situation looks like. A few years ago, I attended one of those Peter Lowe Success Seminars in Orlando. It was an all-day event with about 17,000 people in the arena. One of the speakers was Mayor Rudy Giuliani and he was talking about optimism in leadership. He told the crowd, "Suppose I said to you, 'Things are bad—real bad. And they're going to get worse—a whole lot worse. In fact, they're going to get really terrible. Now follow me!'" Then he said, "Maybe one or two of you will get out of your seat to follow me, because you want my book signed—but no one else would get out of their seats. A leader has to be optimistic simply because if he isn't, nobody else will be."

Lincoln Lessons for Today
Wisdom to Apply Right Now

1. **Realize that paradigm shifts—fundamental changes in the way things are done—occur continually.** Keep yourself razor sharp and ready to be on the cutting edge the next time the plates move. If you don't, you'll wake up one day and wonder where your next job is coming from, with all your marketable skills behind you.

2. **Banish the expression, "We've always done it this way."** Be open to new methods and processes. "New" does not equal "bad."

3. **Instead of fighting change, learn how to use it to your best end.** The world is constantly changing so there's no use resisting it. Instead, keep your ear to the ground and figure out which direction the change is coming from. Then find a way to ride the wave.

4. **Always be optimistic!** No one wants to follow the fellow whose life screams, "Things are bad and getting worse."

CHAPTER 15:

DEVELOP YOUR INNER POWERS

....

Lincoln's Logs, by Gene Griessman

I always enjoyed travelling. When I rode the judicial circuit, I actually enjoyed the journey itself, even though the accommodations were often primitive and the roads sometimes so muddy they were almost impassable. But the experience of getting out, riding on the vast prairies, was a joy to me.

There was one journey that I often took, and it was the most pleasant and rewarding of all. It was the journey within, when I examined my ideas, learned to understand myself, and developed my inner powers. Let me recommend that journey to you.

An axe was put in my hands when I was just a child to clear forests and split rails. Physical strength was important on the frontier.

Permit me to boast a little. Even after I became President, I could extend my arm with a heavy axe and sustain it horizontally, something most young men could not do.

But there is a strength that is more important for a leader than physical strength. That strength derives from your inner powers.

Let me say a few words about developing your inner powers.

• *Developing your inner powers involves learning to make difficult decisions.*

When you attempt virtually any project, there will be good and bad outcomes. You can seldom be certain which will occur, good or bad, or how much of either will occur.

But you can *learn to think in terms of probabilities.* You decide in advance what are the best outcomes, and what you are prepared to pay in order to get those outcomes. When you are making a difficult decision, *look for and find the one essential thing.*

That may sound too theoretical, but it is an imminently practical idea that I regularly employed when I was trying a case as a lawyer. We decided in advance what the client absolutely had to get out of the case. I knew that I was most likely to get that one thing if I was prepared to concede what was not crucial.

Once when I was trying a case on the judicial circuit, our opponent made one claim after another. Each time, I said, "I'll give you that." I did that so many times that my client became anxious and whispered, "My God, Lincoln, you're giving away the entire case." But I knew in advance what we had to get, and I got it.

The true rule in determining to embrace or reject anything is not whether it has any evil in it, but whether it has more of evil than of good. There are few things wholly evil or wholly good. Almost everything is an inseparable compound of the two, so that our best judgment of the preponderance between them is continually demanded.

– A. LINCOLN

The hardest decision I had to make was whether the Union was worth fighting for, whether the future of people's government was worth the blood that was being shed, whether I should make peace and allow the slaves who had been freed to become slaves again.

I could have stopped the killing any day with one stroke of my pen. I made the decision that saving the union and people's government and the emancipated slaves was a prize that could not be conceded. I hope that you will never have to make a decision of that magnitude.

- *Developing your inner powers involves being resolute.*

Make it your goal to be known as a resolute person. This does not mean that you cannot be flexible. The willow tree survives great storms that destroy mighty oaks because the willow tree bends but does not break. I suppose I was more like a willow tree than an oak, much of the time. But I did not break. I take some pride in saying that during my term of office, the American flag did not lose one single star. You are not likely to become a leader if your followers cannot trust you to be steadfast.

Developing your inner powers involves using your subconscious mind.

Intuition—that deep and mysterious decision-making ability of the mind—is sometimes called the subconscious or the unconscious mind. Whatever you call it, it is a powerful force that is often unused or misused.

Learn to tap into its awesome power. You will find that your sub-conscious can solve problems for you while you sleep or while you work at something else.

But do not misuse intuition. There are few things more dangerous than an ignorant man trusting his intuition. *Intuition is most valuable when it is deeply informed. Immerse yourself in the subject, and then let your intuition do its work.*

Ralph Waldo Emerson put it this way, "Learn to detect and watch that gleam of light which flashes across the mind from within...Do not dismiss without notice your own ideas, just because they are your own. Trust yourself," he said. "Great minds have always done so...."

• *Developing your inner powers involves protecting yourself.*

Protect your inner spirit, for it is fragile. You may seem tough and resilient on the outside, but in your heart, you know that you are vulnerable. If an enemy can get past your defenses, the enemy can destroy your good ideas and may steal your joy. I wonder just how many great ideas have been killed with a laugh or a sneer or a discouraging word?

Create defenses that are formidable so that only those you know and trust can get inside. Do not allow yourself to become an open book that anyone can read. I wrote "confidential" on many of my letters because I did not want my privacy invaded.

Will springs from the two elements of moral sense and self-interest.

– A. LINCOLN

Do not tell just anyone what you plan to do. Do it first. It does not hurt a leader to be known as mysterious and inscrutable. Men freely ford a stream if they can easily see its bed.

I learned to *seem* open and gregarious, telling stories, joking and laughing freely, but revealing only what I wanted to reveal.

Toward the end of my first term I wrote: "If, at the end, when I come to lay down the reins of power, I have lost every other friend on earth, I shall at least have one friend left, and that friend shall be deep down inside of me....I am not bound to win, but I am bound to be true. I am not bound to succeed, but I am bound to live up to the light I have."

On another occasion, one of my people asked me if I was going to reply to a particularly hurtful criticism. I answered, "If I tried to read, much less answer, all the attacks on me, I would have no time for any other business. I do the very best I know how--the very best I can; and I mean to keep doing so until the end.

"If the end brings me out right, what is said against me won't amount to anything. If the end brings me out wrong, ten angels swearing I was right would make no difference."

Living Lincoln: Develop Your Inner Powers
By Pat Williams

Physical strength mattered on the prairie. But for a contemporary leader, as it was for Lincoln himself, there's a strength more important than physical—and it comes from your inner powers. Let's talk about how we can practically apply Lincoln's "inner power" principles to our lives today.

1. Learning to make difficult decisions. While the words "evil" and "good" may not be part of your business vocabulary, what Lincoln says is nevertheless accurate. Every choice before us has both elements within it—like a two-sided coin.

In early 1964, I signed up for the Army Reserves. I'll be totally upfront about it: I had a career in professional baseball that was underway, and I didn't want to go to Vietnam, where war was raging. Military service was required in those days and by joining the reserves, I avoided the dreaded draft.

I spent the 1964 baseball season working in the front office of the Philadelphia Phillies farm club in Miami, Florida. It was a wonderful season for me personally—and a *great* year for the big club in Philadelphia. They were on their way to playing in the World Series, and everyone was rejoicing.

In late August of '64, I got two letters on back-to-back days. The first was from the Phillies, inviting me to come to Philadelphia in September to help prepare for the World Series. *Wow! I was going to the Big Leagues.*

The next day, I received a letter from Uncle Sam, instructing me to report to Ft. Jackson, South Carolina on September 12, to start my basic training.

So long, Philadelphia! No Big Leagues!

And as it turned out, there was no World Series, as in one of the most dramatic collapses ever, the Phillies faded coming down the stretch and didn't make it. And by that time I was lugging a rifle around Ft. Jackson and down on the ground doing pushups.

But I'd had a tough decision to make regarding my attitude. Like many young soldiers during the Civil War and in any time of conflict, I didn't want to go!

Today, I am very proud of my military service. Every Memorial Day at our church, First Baptist Orlando, the pastor asks all military veterans to stand and be recognized. I always get to do that. I will never be mistaken for a military hero, but I am extremely proud that I wore the uniform of my country, back in my younger days.

When you're faced with a difficult decision, as I was—maybe it's about whether or not to lay off a valuable employee, or a possible acquisition—remember that two-sided coin. Then ask yourself, what is the one essential thing—the one non-negotiable outcome? For me, it was avoiding an unwanted trip overseas, and we all know today what Lincoln saw as the one essential thing. We owe so much of our freedom today to Lincoln's difficult decision.

2. Becoming resolute. Effective leaders must be men and women their followers can trust to be steadfast. Are you determined regarding enforcement of your policies and decisions? No one wants to follow a leader who vacillates, testing their daily decisions with the direction of the wind. How many times in political contests do we hear about candidates who flip-flop? It's enough to make you dizzy. Be firm in your positions and resolute in your resolve. Yes, even Lincoln was known to change his mind in the face of new information—but let it be a sign of strength based on expanded understanding and not of waffling weakness.

3. Using your subconscious mind. Are you even aware of that part of you? Most of us today are so pre-occupied with noise or running from meeting to meeting, we take little time to connect with ourselves. Lincoln especially advises us to "inform our subconscious mind." We do that by acquiring information that will help us make that decision. Do you need to consult others? Read a book? What can you do to make sure you have all the facts?

A colleague of mine told me about a time she sat on a jury for a criminal trial. The initial case was made and the witnesses were interviewed—two eyewitnesses and a few character witnesses. The attorneys—a raw public prosecutor and a slick defense attorney—made their respective cases. The defense attorney did his best to blow smoke into the picture and by the time the jury was sequestered, they were about ready to buy his story. Instead, they adjourned and agreed to meet the next day for a decision.

Somewhere in those intervening hours, it became clear to my friend that the defendant was, indeed, guilty as charged. Her subconscious had been informed and her intuition did the rest. Next day, she made her case to her fellow jurors and they agreed. As a result a young criminal was taken off the streets—hopefully in time to turn his life around. What verdict do you need to reach? Make sure you get all the facts and then trust your "intuition."

4. Protecting yourself. In sports, we call this "putting on your game face." Never let your opponent know what you're thinking or planning. Let me take you back to one of the great moments in NBA history, the seventh game of the 1970 NBA finals.

The Los Angeles Lakers and the New York Knicks were tied at three games apiece, and it was game seven, at Madison Square Garden in New York. One huge issue that night surrounded Willis Reed, the Knicks' great center, who had a severely injured knee. Would he suit up? Was he even capable of playing? The Knicks' front office and coaching staff didn't say a word. There was lots of conjecture, but the Knicks were stone-faced.

About five minutes before game time, Willis Reed limped out, alone. The eruption in the Garden was electrifying. It turned the whole climate around. Willis was hobbled and was not able to play to full capacity, but he hit two jump shots early in the game and so ignited the fan base, the Lakers never could recover. The Knicks won the championship in a route, and to this day it was more emotion than anything else that helped win the title.

Lincoln Lessons for Today

Wisdom to Apply Right Now

1. **Develop your inner strength**—it will serve you better than physical strength during times of conflict and trial.

2. **Learn to make difficult decisions.** What's the one essential outcome you need from the situation? Consider how best to achieve that end.

3. **Be resolute.** People won't follow a leader they can't trust for long, and that means being yourself—not a weak imitation of someone else. Be flexible when necessary, but hold your ground

4. **Use your subconscious mind.** Gather the information you need to inform your decision and then trust yourself to see the answer clearly. Give the picture time to come into focus.

5. **Protect yourself.** If you're going to be an open book, make sure you're on a private library shelf. Choose carefully those with whom you will share your thoughts and feelings.

CHAPTER 16:

WHAT LIFE IS MADE OF

....

Lincoln's Logs, by Gene Griessman

I always enjoyed reading *Poor Richard's Almanac* by Benjamin Franklin. One old issue contained this maxim: "Dost thou love life? Then do not squander time, for that is the stuff life is made of."

In that same *Almanac* are the words: "Plough deep while sluggards sleep." And in a little book he wrote entitled *Advice to a Young Tradesman*, Franklin said: "Remember that time is money."

The books I read in school were full of sayings like the sayings of Poor Richard, which reminded us that idleness was bad, and life was precious. Here's one of them: "The devil tempts most people, but an idle person tempts the devil."

I took all those sayings to heart. Time-consciousness became a way of life for me.

I already told you about the poem I memorized when I was just a youth [in full in chapter 19].

"Oh! why should the spirit of mortal be proud?

Like a swift-fleeing meteor, a fast-flying cloud,

A flash of the lightning, a break of the wave,

He passeth from life to his rest in the grave."

I thought a lot about how brief life is. I had many reminders. My infant brother, Thomas, died in childbirth. My sister Sarah died shortly after she was married. My dear friend Ann Rutledge died when she was just twenty-two. We lost our first son, little Eddie, when he was just a wee lad. It broke my heart. His mother and I counted the days he was with us and had them engraved on his little tombstone: three years, ten months, and eighteen days.

Sometimes I hear people say, "I'll sure be glad when this week is over," and I think, "What a foolish thing to say—to wish away a precious gift." Valuing time is the start of a good habit—but you must do more than simply value time if you wish to be successful.

I account partially for his kindness to me because of the similarity with which I had fought my way up, we both starting at the lowest round of the ladder.

— FREDERICK DOUGLASS,
FORMER SLAVE WHO BECAME AN INTERNATIONALLY
CELEBRATED EDITOR AND ORATOR

You must learn to be diligent in the use of time. Here's some advice I gave lawyers: "The leading rule for the lawyer, as for the man of every calling, is diligence. Leave nothing for tomorrow which can be done today. Never let your correspondence fall behind. Whatever piece of business you have in hand, before stopping, do all the labor pertaining to it which can then be done."

Time is life. Unfortunately, most people do not value it properly until they realize that they are running out of it.

Be judicious about what you choose to do. If a thing is not worth doing, be sure not to do it.

Be strategic about your time. Know what can be best done at your leisure, or not done at all, and what cannot be put off.

If you choose to do something, do it with all the skill and care that you possess. Benjamin Franklin took as his motto a verse from the Bible, which I have taken to heart as well: "Seest thou a man diligent in his business? He shall stand before kings…."

The most successful man in the world has one thing in common with the most unsuccessful man in the world. Both have twenty-four hour days. The difference between them is what they do with those twenty-four hours.

The duration of a life or reign is contracted to a fleeting moment: the grave is ever beside the throne.

– From a favorite Lincoln passage by Edward Gibbon, *The History of the Decline and Fall of the Roman Empire*

Living Lincoln: What Life is Made Of
By Pat Williams

Lincoln understood that life was short, even without knowing his own would be abbreviated by an assassin's bullet. He was wise to study the lessons of Ben Franklin—a man whose advice applies to us today as well.

Speaking of Franklin, on September 20, 1995, I had a life-changing experience. The Orlando Magic had a daylong seminar before the start of the season. We were out on Disney property. We went through the morning session, broke for lunch, and then in the afternoon session a pert little blonde in a cream-colored suit appeared on the stage. Her name was Ruth Hanchey and she was a trainer for the FranklinCovey organization. She taught time-management and organizational skills— how to use your Franklin Planner to get your life together.

At that time I was fifty-five years old and had been in professional sports since I was twenty-two. Basically, while I did have a calendar pad on my desk in the office, all my appointments, phone messages—everything—were written on the back of a torn envelope or a piece of scratch paper I'd grabbed somewhere along the way. My life was filled with all sorts of notes, flying in every direction.

Abraham Lincoln once said, "The habit of uselessly wasting time is the whole difficulty; and it is vastly important...that you should break this habit." I hadn't signed up for it, but I was about to find out how to do exactly that.

I'd never heard of the FranklinCovey Company or the concept of time management. Ruth put on a four-hour seminar that day that was absolutely mind-blowing. She taught us how to lay our days out, our weeks out, our months out—using this thing. She even had a chant that went, "How often should you have your Franklin Planner with you?" And the audience would respond, "Always!" It was a turning point day for me. To this day, I've got every year since 1995 in bound cases on my shelves. Every phone call I've made since September of 1995, everything that's happened every day for the last thirteen years—it's all there, tucked away. My entire life is glued together like a giant puzzle.

As it happened, I'd just finished a book called *Go for the Magic*[3] (Thomas Nelson 1995) about Walt Disney's five secrets of success. When the program was over I went up and introduced myself to Ruth. I told her I had a new book out and would love to give her a copy, which I did. We talked in the parking lot. I found out she was single, as was I at the time. I

---

3   Walt's secrets? They worked magic for Walt, and they'll work for anyone: 1) Think "tomorrow," or how to build the rest of your life; 2) free your imagination with blue-sky thinking; 3) strive for lasting quality; 4) have "stick-to-it-ivity"—stubbornness with a purpose; and 5) have fun!

did have a little baggage—eighteen children. I remember Ruth said to me, "I've always wanted more children," and I thought, *Well, I can fix that!*

To make a long story short, in April of 1997 I married the Franklin Planner lady—and added one more child in the bargain. Without a doubt that's the best decision I ever made. Ruth teaches me every day to treasure what life is made of, and believe me, it slips through our fingers all too quickly.

Lincoln Lessons for Today
Wisdom to Apply Right Now

1. Do you love life? Most of us do. If you do too, then think every day about Ben Franklin's wisdom—**don't squander the time you've been given!**

2. **Be diligent in learning how to wisely use your time.** Time management requires more than good intentions. It requires a systematic plan and the use of proven time-management principles. If you need help, I can recommend a fabulous FranklinCovey trainer.

3. **Be wise in the way you invest your time.** Avoid activities that are not adding to your life in some way. Remember those words Lincoln quoted, originally spoken by Solomon, the wisest man in the world in his time, "Seest thou a man diligent in his business? He shall stand before kings; he shall not stand before mean men" (Proverbs 22:29 KJV). To Franklin, this signified the fact that he, himself, had been honored by men of high station; Lincoln would be in years to come. Take up their legacy—make it your goal to stand before kings.

CHAPTER 17:

YOUR NAME IS YOUR BRAND

....

Lincoln's Logs, by Gene Griessman

I'm not sure just how I came to be known as "Honest Abe." Maybe it's because I have a lazy streak in me, and I realized that telling lies is hard work.

It requires a considerable amount of mental effort to think up a lie that people will believe. And it requires additional effort to tell a lie convincingly—to appear to be telling the truth, when you're not.

Additional effort is required for you to remember exactly how you told the lie down to the smallest detail—forever. You never know when someone will ask you about it. That's mentally tiring and stressful, to have to be on your guard.

So I decided it's easier to tell the truth, and be done with it.

As you would put it today, "Honest Abe" became my brand.

It's really an old idea. Shakespeare wrote: "Who steals my purse steals trash; 'tis something, nothing; 'Twas mine, 'tis his, and has been slave to thousands; But he that filches from me my good name robs me of that which not enriches him, and makes me poor indeed."

I resolved to be an honest lawyer.

Oh, I know the lawyer jokes. They told them in the 1800s, too.

Like the story about two women at a funeral: The minister said, "Here lies a lawyer, and an honest man." One woman said to another: "Do you suppose there're two bodies in that casket?"

Here's advice that I gave to young lawyers: "If, in your own judgment, you cannot be an honest lawyer, resolve to be honest without being a lawyer. Choose some other occupation, rather than one in the choosing of which you do, in advance, consent to be a knave."

If you're dishonest long enough, you're going to get caught. You can fool all of the people some of the time, and some of the people all the time, but you can't fool all of the people all of the time.

I have always wanted to deal with everyone I meet candidly and honestly. If I have made any assertion not warranted by facts, and it is pointed out to me, I will withdraw it cheerfully.

— A. LINCOLN

Shakespeare again: "This above all: to thine own self be true, and it must follow, as the night the day, Thou cans't not then be false to any man."

Being honest doesn't mean that you have to be naïve. There's something more important than knowing the truth, and that's knowing what to do with the truth.

Being wise involves knowing when to tell the truth, how to tell the truth, who to tell the truth to. The village idiot might stumble upon the truth, tell everybody in sight, and do irreparable damage. Some truths you should never tell—like when your wife asks you what you really think about her new dress—which you think is ugly. Always tell the truth, but don't always be telling it.

Let me tell you a fable that illustrates the point. There once was a great king, who when he was old and going blind, decided to make one last trip to visit his distant domains. Before leaving he called into his presence one of his generals who had distinguished himself on the battlefield. "I have heard of your exploits," the king said, "and I would like you to oversee an important project.

"On the beautiful mountain there, I want you to build a great castle. You will have unlimited funds at your disposal. Spare no expense. Find the greatest architect, the finest marble, mother of pearl, alabaster and rare timbers. Use the most skillful artisans. Make it a fabulous place. Will you do that for me?"

The general agreed, and some days later the king departed.

No sooner was the king gone that the general said, "It is wasteful to build another castle. He already has more than he can visit. So the general chose an inexperienced architect and incompetent artisans, and substituted cheap materials. Instead of marble, he chose plaster; instead of embedded jewels, worthless stones. "The king is almost blind. He will never know," thought the general.

By and by the king returned and in due time called the general into his presence. "Is the palace finished?"

"Yes, your highness."

"Is it a fabulous place?"

"Yes, your highness."

"Did you construct it exactly the way I requested—with the finest design, the most skilled craftsmen, the richest materials?"

"Yes, your highness. Would you like to see the castle?"

"See the castle? No, I have more castles that I can ever visit. Besides, I trust you. That castle is my reward for your brave service. It is my gift to you."

Do I need to tell you the moral of that story? Perhaps.

When you decide to cheat someone else, you may end up cheating yourself.

Another possible lesson. You must live in the house that you build.

I am happy that I came to be known as Honest Abe. It has been a good brand. My career would have been far different had I come to be known as Crooked Abe.

Mr. Lincoln's judgment was final in all that region of country. People relied implicitly on his honesty, integrity, and impartiality.

– R.B. RUTLEDGE,
NEW SALEM RESIDENT AND BROTHER OF ANN RUTLEDGE

Living Lincoln: Your Name is Your Brand
By Pat Williams

It was that same Shakespeare Lincoln refers to who also wrote in his famous story of star-crossed lovers, Romeo and Juliet, "What's in a name? That which we call a rose by any other name would smell as sweet." And his reasoning cannot really be argued with. But in today's world, names do carry a lot of weight.

There is much being said about branding these days, and none of it has anything to do with cattle. Today, corporate branding involves making yourself known for something. It means building brand loyalty, being easily identified and well known. Let me just argue here that it all begins with your personal brand. What kind of leader are you? What are you— just you—known for?

Back when I was involved with starting up Orlando's NBA expansion team, I knew we had to find a dynamite name—something that would set us apart from the pack. We needed a name that was as fresh and new as our team would be—something that tied us to the community while spelling out s-t-r-e-n-g-t-h on the scoreboard. What should it be? Anyone who's ever been a parent recognizes how a name becomes a part of one's identity.

To help us out, the local paper, the Orlando *Sentinel,* held a name-the-team contest—hauling in over 4,000 entries. After crawling out from under the pile, we proceeded to weed them and weigh them. At last, it came down to four possibilities: Juice, Heat, Magic, and Tropics. All of them seemed appropriate for this region. But only one of them really seemed to capture what I had sensed ever since I'd first arrived in Orlando. What happened on the Sunday before "naming day" nailed it.

It was my then-seven-year-old daughter Karyn's birthday, so I flew her from our home in New Jersey to Orlando for a big celebration—and we did it all. Disney World, Sea World—everything the town had to offer. When it was over, Karyn said, "Daddy, it's so wonderful here! This place is magic!" That is when it became crystal clear to me.

From the moment I'd first set foot in Orlando, there was no doubt about the "brand" that had consumed that community. Walt Disney, who had never even lived there, was everywhere. The power of one man's personality, translated into Walt Disney World, was undeniably alive. Magic was literally in the air. Before Walt Disney arrived, Orlando had been a sleepy orange grove community. Today, it is a bustling, thriving hub of activity—magically alive.

And so, Magic it was—the joyful kind of magic that embodied Orlando.

Your brand, whatever it is, needs to reflect who you are. For us, the name "Magic" suggested the essence of Central Florida and all it had to offer, the wonders that had drawn Walt Disney to build his Magic Kingdom there in the first place.

Would we have thought "Magic" was such a great name if Walt Disney had not lived such a remarkable life? It's hard to say, but one thing is certain—Walt, always ahead of his time, understood what it meant to base your reputation on a "brand." In his company's case it was to be known for providing the finest in family entertainment. Everything Walt did during his entire abbreviated life was focused on building and protecting that brand.

What about you? Are you known in your office, church, school, synagogue, military unit, mosque, temple, or community as an "Honest Abe" or a "Magical Walt"? Whatever you are known for, make sure that, as a leader, your name becomes legendary for all the right reasons.

Lincoln Lessons for Today
Wisdom to Apply Right Now

1. **Have a name known for honesty.** Know what to do with the truth. If you do, no one will ever doubt your word.

2. **Have a name known for wisdom.** Know when to tell the truth.

3. **Have a name known for integrity.** Ken Whitten, who is coach Tony Dungy's pastor in Tampa, Florida, told me recently, "The tongue in Tony's mouth is always pointing in the same direction as the tongue in Tony's shoes." That is a life of integrity. It's a brand worth having.

CHAPTER 18:

HARNESSING DEPRESSION

....

Lincoln's Logs, by Gene Griessman

Recently a man asked me if I could be elected President today, and I told him "no." He wanted to know why. Because I had two nervous breakdowns, I told him, and after the digging-up-dirt machine got through with me, people would conclude that I was emotionally unfit to be President.

Just to make my point, a few decades ago [1972] there was a Senator from Missouri by the name of Thomas Eagleton who was chosen by his party as their nominee for Vice President. He was actually put on the ticket, but they kicked him off the ticket when they learned that he had required treatment for depression.

That standard would eliminate me.

I have been encouraged to talk about my depression because literally millions of people are afflicted by it. Many of them are quite successful and do their best to hide their problem. Winston Churchill had severe bouts of depression. He called his problem "the black dog."

There are three possible outcomes for severe depression:

1. You can be overcome by it. You won't be able to keep functioning. You won't want to get up in the morning. Just talking will be a chore. You may do yourself in. There were two times in my life when my friends had a suicide watch for me.

2. You can learn to live with it—with medicine and therapy.

3. You can learn to harness this powerful energy and channel it in creative, useful ways.

I'm not sure what the source of my depression was. Some said it was heredity. There's no doubt that some of the Lincolns were a bit off center. My father often had bouts of the blues. My mother was kind, and tender, mild and—sad. One of my uncles had what he called "the Lincoln horrors." One of my cousins died in a mental institution.

I understand that my genes did not give me the disease, just a susceptibility to it.

Some people said it was because so many people around me died. My baby brother died when I was three; my mother died when I was nine. My big sister Sarah who had helped raise me after mother died and was my best friend died when I was just eighteen. After she was gone, I felt so lonely I cried, inside.

And then there was Ann—Ann Rutledge who died of a fever when I was a young man in New Salem, Illinois. She was just twenty-two. But I already told you that.

After I married, we lost little Eddie. He lay ill for fifty-two days. Mary and I wrote a poem which The Illinois State *Journal* published a week after we buried him:

> *Those midnight stars are sadly dimmed,*
> *That late so brilliantly shone,*
> *And the crimson tinge from cheek and lip,*
> *With the heart's warm life has flown -*
> *The angel of Death was hovering nigh,*
> *And the lovely boy was called to die....*
>
> *Angel Boy - fare thee well, farewell*

Sweet Eddie, We bid thee adieu!
Affection's wail cannot reach thee now
Deep though it be, and true.
Bright is the home to him now given
For "of such is the Kingdom of Heaven."

We put these words on his little gravestone—"Of Such is the Kingdom of Heaven."

And then there was Willie, dear sweet Willie. He was just eleven. He died in the White House. Willie was too good for this earth…and we loved him so. Losing Willie was the hardest trial of my life.

> According to psychiatrist George Vaillant, Lincoln effectively used at least five powerful techniques to deal with his depression. 1) Humor – he loved to tell jokes; 2) suppression – he selectively pushed away thoughts that oppressed him; 3) anticipation – Lincoln forced himself to recognize that the gloom would pass and he would soon feel better; 4) altruism – he taught himself to live in such a way that his life would benefit his fellow man; 5) sublimation – he channeled his emotions into art—writing speeches and poetry.
>
> – GENE GRIESSMAN

Some people have speculated that my depression came from my troubled, difficult relations with my father. There is not doubt that he never understood me, and sometimes treated me roughly. We were never close.

Sociologists might say that I am what they call a marginal man—someone caught between two worlds. It's true that I was caught between the world I decided to leave, which was filled with simple, uneducated manual workers—and the world of well-schooled, well-off people, many of whom never fully accepted me.

My past was an embarrassment to me. I didn't want to talk about it. Now I am praised for having risen from the lowest strata of society, but it was humiliating then for people to know what I came from.

The men would start talking about going to college, and the women would talk about going to finishing schools, and I, I had gone to school a total of about one year. You can imagine how mortified I felt.

I was caught in the middle. I wanted to be like people who went to college and had money, but those people never fully accepted me. One of my cabinet officers called me a first-rate fourth-rate man. Another one, when he read that a famous adventurer of the times was going to some far-off land to capture a rare gorilla, said that the man could have saved himself a lot of time and money because there was a fine specimen in the White House. I laughed when I heard it, but it hurt.

It has never been easy for me to be looked down on. I always wanted to be respected and taken seriously.

But in an ironic way, my melancholy helped me to be taken seriously.

People began to take me seriously because there was a sad side to me. Some even said I had gravitas—a seriousness that caused them to respect me. But that is getting ahead of my story.

There were the whispers about me and my family. They whispered that my mother was illegitimate and that I probably was too. People called the Hanks and the Sparrows and the Lincolns "white trash."

Rising from the lower class is romantic only if you're the teller of the tale, not if you're the one who's doing the rising.

What was it that caused these dark spells that came over me? I don't know for sure. Whatever the cause, it hurt—a lot.

So what did I do?

• *I sought treatment, professional treatment—and I recommend that to you.*

It is now known that depression can result from a chemical imbalance that can be helped with medicine, or from other issues that can be helped through counseling.

In my day, the treatment was harsh and primitive. Commonly patients were bled, and purged, thinking that would restore the balance of upset humors. They wanted to get the bad blood out of me. It didn't work, so in some ways I had to become my own psychiatrist.

I learned that there were techniques I could use that would help me break loose from the hold that depression had on me. Here are some of the best ones:

• *I found friends who cared about me, friends who were bright and cheerful.*

Ward Lamon was a wild man, who liked to drink, sing, and carouse. He was the opposite of me. Many of my friends criticized me for associating with someone so disreputable, but Lamon was good for me. He cheered me up.

• *I told jokes.*

A funny story, if it has the element of genuine wit, puts new life into me.

Laughter was my medicine perhaps because I laughed at my own jokes. If it were not for those stories—jokes—I should have died. They give vent to my moods and gloom.

I sometimes would begin a cabinet meeting by reading aloud something humorous from the newspaper. My favorite humorist was David Ross Locke, who wrote under the name of Petroleum Vesuvius Nasby. Even his pen name sounded funny to me. Or I would tell a funny story. Several of my cabinet members asked me how could I tell a joke when all the news from the front was bad. I told them, I laugh to keep from crying.

I am not like some of your comedians today who tell jokes and don't laugh. I laugh at my own stories because I tell them to help *me*, not just to amuse those who listen to me. Sometimes I'm telling them for myself. If others laugh, that's a bonus.

Laughter is the joyous, beautiful, universal evergreen of life.

— A. LINCOLN

• *I read the Bible.*

I'm a pretty unorthodox man when it comes to religion, but once when I was having a severe bout of depression the mother of Joshua Speed gave me a copy of the Bible. She showed me some passages to read when I felt blue. I particularly benefited from reading the Book of Job.

• *I gradually learned that I soon would be better again.*

Young people don't know this, the first time depression hits them, and I didn't know it either the first time. It didn't seem like the sun would ever shine again, but just like a terrible storm, it passed, and the sun did shine again. The next time it happened I told myself, *It will soon be over. Even this shall pass.* In the depth and even agony of despondency, I understood that very shortly I would feel well again.

- *I looked for something to do, even if it seemed unimportant at the time.*

Here's what I wrote to Joshua Speed, my best friend, who suffered from melancholia too: "Avoid being idle; I would immediately engage in some business, or go to making preparations for it."

- *Refuse to brood over slights.*

Here's something else I wrote: "Jealousy and suspicion never did help any man in any situation. There may sometimes be ungenerous attempts to keep a young man down, and they will succeed, too, if he allows his mind to be diverted from its true channel to brood over the attempted injury. Cast about, and see if this feeling has not injured every person you have ever known to fall into it."

- *Find time to be quiet and alone.*

Often in the White House, after official business had ended, I would shut the door and would sometimes sit for long periods of time, in complete silence, with my eyes almost shut. By looking inward, I found the strength to continue.

The losses on either side at Chancellorsville were severe. That evening I believed myself to be alone in the Executive Mansion, except for the President in his room across the hall...

A dull, regularly repeated sound came out of Lincoln's room through its half-open door. I became aware that this was the measured tread of the President's feet, as he walked steadily to and fro, up and down, on the farther side...

Two o'clock in the morning came, and Lincoln was walking still. It was a vigil with God and with the future, and a long wrestle with disaster and, it may be, with himself.

It was almost three o'clock when I arose to go. I listened before going down, and the last sound that I heard was the sentry-like tread with which the President was marching.

It was not yet eight o'clock in the morning when I was once more at the White House. On reaching the second floor, I saw the President's door wide open and looked in.

There he sat, near the end of the Cabinet table, with a breakfast before him. Just beyond the cup of coffee at his right lay a sheet of paper, covered with fresh writing in his own hand. They were the orders under which General Meade shortly took (General Joe) Hooker's place and marched on to Gettysburg.

That long night and combat had been a victory, for he turned to me with a bright and smiling face and talked with me as cheerfully as if he had not been up all night in that room, face-to-face with Chancellorsville."

— WILLIAM OSBORN STODDARD,
ONE OF LINCOLN'S THREE PERSONAL SECRETARIES IN THE WHITE
HOUSE, ABBREVIATED AND EXCERPTED FROM *INTIMATE MEMORIES OF
LINCOLN*, ASSEMBLED AND ANNOTATED BY RUFUS ROCKWELL WILSON,
ELMIRA, NY, THE PRIMAVERA PRESS, 1945, PP. 238, 239

- *Find something bigger than yourself to live for.*

Years before I arrived at the White House, I told Joshua Speed, "I have an irrepressible desire to accomplish something that will link my name with something that will redound to the interest of my fellow man."

After I signed the Emancipation Proclamation, I wrote to Speed and reminded him of what I had written years before. I told him that now, finally, I had done something that would redound to the benefit of my fellow man.

Living Lincoln: Harnessing Depression
By Pat Williams

Can you imagine what would happen today if we had a political candidate for high office who'd been known to have even one mental breakdown? Our 24/7 news culture and the fringe slime machines would have a field day—and the poor candidate would not likely stand a chance of being anything other than ridiculed.

Yet many people suffer from depression or other emotional issues. It's really nothing new, nor is it likely to go away through medication. Mental and emotional issues are tricky. I don't claim to be an expert on them in any way, but I can tell you that with a family as large as mine I've certainly seen just about every kind of manifestation of emotions there is.

The classic case of emotional breakdown in professional sports involved baseball player Jimmy Piersall, who played centerfield in the 1950s for the Boston Red Sox. Piersall was a wonderful talent, but emotionally and mentally he just couldn't keep it together, and had to leave the game for awhile. He required professional help, but eventually he was able to resume his career, becoming a longtime broadcaster and also a coach.

His 1957 autobiography written with Al Hirshberg, *Fear Stikes Out*, led to a movie that year of the same name, starring Tony Perkins (*Psycho*) as Piersall. It's instructive to watch it. Piersall's story inspires me to believe that there is almost no adversity, no state of depression, no trial that cannot be overcome if we determine to claim ultimate victory.

What was Lincoln's secret for overcoming depression, and how can we employ it today to keep ourselves from being dragged down by it, or rendered ineffective by a black cloud in our mind? How can we learn to harness our emotions as Lincoln did?

Every one of the points Lincoln made are just as valid today as they were in his era.

1. He found friends who cared about him and who had bright and cheerful personalities. The last thing a depressed person needs is company that loves misery. If I had a personal "brand" like "Honest Abe," it would probably be "Positive Pat." I'm a generally upbeat sort of guy, so I can't claim to know a lot about depression. But I can recall a terribly dark season in my life—it began when my first wife, Jill, moved out.

Long dissatisfied with our marriage, her departure left me feeling like a failure. As a leader—not only in sports, but in my community and in my church—I was ashamed and embarrassed by this divorce. How could I tell my friends? But when I finally did open up—at first at dinner to some close friends—I was stunned to discover not rejection—but love! They felt my hurt with me, they prayed with me, and loved me.

Thanks to these friends and so many more, I found new hope to go on in the face of despair. I urge you to find friends like mine and like Lincoln's—friends who support you, encourage you, and help you become all you are meant to be. I call them Life Enhancers, and everybody needs them.

2. Lincoln told jokes, and he laughed when others told them. Laughter is a well-known medicine. If the news is bad, do what Lincoln did and find a reason to laugh—it will keep you from crying.

A few years ago, I put together a book with my dear friend Ken Hussar called *Winning with One-Liners* (Health Communications 2002), and in it I offer a sizeable collection of lines proven to get laughs when included in speeches. Ken and I have been collecting one-line humor for over thirty years and we never tire of chortling over our latest finds. Like the one about the major league pitcher who's been having a bad season: "He's working on a new pitch. It's called a strike." Or the one about the short basketball player: "He's so short he needs to stand on a stool while showering. Otherwise the water would be cold by the time it reached him." Of course, those used to working in a pressure-cooker environment relate to this one and it always leaves them laughing: "We have a tough sick leave policy. There is no time off for illness or surgery. Death is accepted but you have to give three weeks' notice."

I've been speaking in public as long as I've been in professional sports and I am here to attest that nothing wins an audience over like a well-told joke. We all love to laugh! Tap into it.

One of the things I've appreciated most about many of the presidents who've served during my lifetime—men like John F. Kennedy, Ronald Reagan, Bill Clinton and George W. Bush—was their ability to laugh at themselves. As leaders, this is a huge plus factor. Learn to laugh at yourself and the world will laugh *with* you, not at you.

3. Lincoln read the Bible, particularly the book of Job. In time, Lincoln learned he would get better, just as life got better for Job. When we're young, we don't know that storms will come to pass in our lives. It takes experience—the living out of life—to teach us that the sun does shine again, eventually.

Like Lincoln, I find tremendous comfort and reassurance from the pages of Scripture. Where else can we find such incomparable words of life, hope, and eternal vision? Nowhere else that I know. Yes, there are books-a-bunch out there on how to find spiritual comfort, but it's my personal view that only the Bible tells me about a God who is the same yesterday, today, and forever. He doesn't sugarcoat reality—life is hard! But his words give me hope for tomorrow, because I know in whose hands it lies. Lincoln knew that same God and found great hope and strength in his Word. I recommend it, and I think Lincoln would too.

4. Lincoln looked for something to do—even if it seemed unimportant at the time. Staying occupied is a good way to keep your mind out of dark corners.

In 1962, my dad was killed in an automobile accident while driving home from my college graduation. It was a shocking development for all of us.

I'd received an opportunity to play in the Phillies system and had wanted to go away and play professional baseball that summer. My mother, recently widowed, insisted that I go. Had she not, I could have gone into a deep depression, but that summer of '62 was so demanding I had to stay focused, busy, and productive. I'm eternally grateful for what my mother did for me that tragic year. She made sure I had something to do other than grieve.

Later on, as a dad with a house full of small children, I witnessed many moments when a child in my house threatened to blow more fiercely than any Florida hurricane—and I never saw it fail that if that child's attention were diverted by something cheerful and fun, the storm would quickly blow over. Oh, there were the stubborn holdouts to be sure. But it's a technique that ultimately wins in the end. If it's so effective with children, how much better can it be for adults who can understand why the change of scenery or activity is beneficial?

5. Refuse to brood. Jealousy never helps any situation. Lincoln discovered firsthand how this truth helped him channel his depression into positive power. In my full household, you can be sure there were many occasions where conflicts and jealousy raged. I don't know many small families who always get along, much less one the size of a major-league baseball team. But time after time, when it looked as if some of my kids had hit a patch they would never get past, I've seen the power of forgiveness come into play. Where is there hurt in your heart? If you truly want to be an effective leader, you've got to let it go.

6. Find time to be quiet and alone. By looking inward, Lincoln says, he found the strength to continue. Even busy executives need to plan these moments of personal "downtime." We all know what it's like to go on offsite trips or team-building excursions. Those are powerful tools! How much more powerful, when it's strength you need, to take time to connect with yourself. Few of us do it in this crazy, non-stop, whirlwind society we live in—but all of us should.

7. Find something bigger than yourself to live for. For Lincoln, it was an "irrepressible desire." For you and me, perhaps it's a desire to leave a legacy, to accomplish something during our time on Earth that will outlive us. For Lincoln, it was signing the Emancipation Proclamation. Maybe you don't have the power to change the world in that way, but all of us can do something to improve life for someone. If you're wealthy, it might be giving your money away to a worthy cause or investing in a research program. If you have time and the inclination, you may want to go on a mission trip to a third-world country. Personally, I can't recommend anything more than adopting a child who needs to know what love is. All of us can do something to prove that, to borrow a phrase from Rick Warren, "It's not about me."

Unlike Lincoln, I am a naturally positive, upbeat person. But I know what it's like when life goes terribly wrong. If we're to survive those sudden storms, we've got to have a battle plan for survival well in advance of that first raindrop. For leaders, this is critical. If we fall apart, so does our team. Let Lincoln's tips move you from the depths of despair to the heights of joy, and learn what it's like to experience a two-fold victory.

Lincoln Lessons for Today
Wisdom to Apply Right Now

1. **Surround yourself with genuine friends**—people who'll have a positive impact on you and lift you up when you're down.
2. **Learn to love laughter.** It's certain to improve your looks—along with your outlook!
3. **Find time to be alone** with yourself and with God to draw strength and wisdom.
4. **Refuse to brood!** When the clouds begin gathering over your heart, blow them away by finding something positive to listen to or do.
5. **Pursue a mission bigger than yourself.**

CHAPTER 19:

TECHNIQUES OF EFFECTIVE COMMUNICATION

....

Lincoln's Logs, by Gene Griessman

There never was a good leader who *wasn't* a great communicator. Fortunately communicating is something that can be learned.

But you have to convince yourself that communicating is important.

It is not enough to work hard, or know a lot about your business, or be technically proficient. It is not enough to make good decisions, as important as that is.

If you make good decisions, you have to be able to communicate your decisions to others in order to gain their acceptance, and support, and the execution of your ideas.

Jefferson Davis, my counterpart in Richmond, was an impressive man—handsome, highly intelligent, with many years of schooling, and considerable experience in the military and national politics. In the South even little children could recite the words, "Jeff Davis rides a snow white horse. Abe Lincoln rides a mule. Jeff Davis is a gentleman. Abe Lincoln is a fool."

Now, Jeff Davis may have ridden a snow white horse, but he was not particularly skillful as a communicator—and that hurt him.

It was a wise man who said: "He who cannot communicate his ideas stands at the same level as he who has no ideas." What does it matter if a leader has a plan that will save his land, if he cannot get his followers to accept it? What does it matter if a physician has a cure for a deadly disease, if he cannot persuade his patients to take it?

If you become a great communicator, there's no telling what you might be able to move. As Archimedes said, "Give me a lever long enough and a place to stand, and I can lift the world."

Communicating well is the way to *multiply* your own individual effort. Communication is your lever.

Few leaders have ever mastered all forms of communication.

Thomas Jefferson gave no more than a handful of public speeches during his two terms as President. But he was a brilliant writer.

Benjamin Franklin was not a great public speaker. He said so himself. But he knew how to write, and influenced tens of thousands with the written word.

George Washington was not a great public speaker, either. But he knew how to speak to small groups, and he knew how to give orders, and he knew how to carry himself, so that when he did say something, he was taken seriously.

Nobody ever becomes a good communicator without effort. It is not something that will happen to you in your sleep.

"Extemporaneous speaking should be practiced and cultivated,"
Lincoln wrote. "It is the lawyer's avenue to the public. However
able and faithful he may be in other respects, people are slow to
bring him business, if he cannot make a speech."

When Lincoln spoke of extemporaneous speaking, he did not
mean making totally unprepared speeches—"winging it"
we might call it today. Few speakers can trust the moment
or their wits alone for a good speech. Very, very few.

- GENE GRIESSMAN

In my day, even in little one-room schools, we were taught rhetoric, which is the study of using language effectively. We learned the rules that the ancients followed to construct their arguments.

We studied a book by Hugh Blair on the subject. Here's what Blair said: "Embarrassed, obscure and feeble sentences are generally, if not always, the result of embarrassed, obscure and feeble thought. Thought and language act and react upon each other mutually.... He that is learning to arrange his sentences with accuracy and order is learning, at the same time, to think with accuracy and order...."

I exposed myself to the biggest ideas and the best communicators I could find. And this is a great success principle:

If you wish to be good at anything, find someone who is good at what you want to do and learn how they do it.

From the time I was a young man, I spent time at the courthouse listening to the lawyers plead their cases.

I read Cicero and Demosthenes, Thomas Paine and Daniel Webster, Robert Burns, William Shakespeare, and the King James Version of the

Bible. I began to feel the rhythms and cadences of the English language. It got in my bones.

I practiced public speaking, sometimes without even knowing I was practicing. When I was a child, sometimes after returning from church, I would assemble my friends on logs and stumps, and deliver a parody of the sermon—much to their delight.

I became a member of a debating society in New Salem. It was a bit like what you call Toastmasters today. We would stand up and give speeches on various topics, and receive critiques. It was good practice.

I learned to tell stories in the evenings in the primitive inns along the route of the judicial circuit. People would come just to listen to the "big dogs" swap stories.

He was the most rapidly logical in any debate and yet he illustrated every point by a humorous anecdote.

– LONGTIME LINCOLN FRIEND
JOSEPH GILLESPIE

When I was growing up in Kentucky and Indiana, the neighbors would come over of an evening, and my father would tell stories. He had no schooling but, oh, Daddy could tell a story. He'd launch into a funny one, and the neighbors would explode with laughter. And then he would tell a sad story and they'd be wiping tears off their cheeks.

I thought to myself, "Daddy's doin' that—with words!" It dawned on me: *words have power.*

Words have been used to encourage and praise me. Words have been used to mock, attack, and wound me. But I have never lost faith in their power or their durability.

Words can reveal thoughts, conceal pain, paint dreams, correct errors, and pass along dearly bought lessons to the latest generation.

Words can transport knowledge from the past, interpret the present, and speak to the future. Words can erect walls between people, or build bridges.

Words can inflame passions or cool them, stir up the worst or find the best, pull down or build up, tarnish or cleanse, wound or heal.

The ability to use words can endear you to your fellows, win them to your side, and help you to rise to heights you may now only dream of. That happened to my father's son.

I determined to be so clear that no honest man
could misunderstand me and no dishonest one
could successfully misrepresent me.

— A. LINCOLN

Pursuing the mastery of words is worth the time, the money, and all the energy you can muster. What you invest will be repaid with interest compounded.

Build up your knowledge so that your words will be true. Nurture your spirit so that your words will be true, kind, and wise.

The world may little note nor long remember what you say here. And yet it may. For words, once released, take on a life of their own, and find lodging in places and hearts you may never know. And after many days, those words may return to haunt you, or to bless you.

Think carefully before you let them go.

Oh! why should the spirit of mortal be proud?
Like a swift-fleeing meteor, a fast-flying cloud,
A flash of the lightning, a break of the wave,
He passeth from life to his rest in the grave.

The leaves of the oak and willow shall fade;
Be scattered around, and together be laid.
And the young and the old, and the low and the high,
Shall moulder to dust, and together shall lie.

The hand of the king that the sceptre hath borne,
The brow of the priest that the mitre hath worn,
The eye of the sage, and the heart of the brave,
Are hidden and lost in the depths of the grave.

The peasant, whose lot was to sow and to reap,
The herdsman, who climbed with his goats up the steep,
The beggar, who wandered in search of his bread,
Have faded away like the grass that we tread.

So the multitude goes--like the flower or the weed,
That withers away to let others succeed;
So the multitude comes--even those we behold,
To repeat every tale that has often been told.

'T is the wink of an eye--'tis the draught of a breath--
From the blossom of health to the paleness of death,
From the gilded saloon to the bier and the shroud:--
Oh! why should the spirit of mortal be proud?[4]

---

4   Mortality, by William Knox, 1789-1825.

Mortality was a favorite poem of mine. I memorized it, and recited it so often that some people thought I wrote it! I would have given anything to have written it.

[Lincoln's] rejection of fine writing was as deliberate as St. Paul's, and for the same reason—because he felt that he was speaking on a subject which must be made clear to the lowest intellect.

— HARRIET BEECHER STOWE,
AUTHOR OF *UNCLE TOM'S CABIN*

Living Lincoln: Effective Communication
By Pat Williams

I've always been fascinated with the spoken word. I can remember, as a youngster growing up in Wilmington, Delaware, attending Tower Hill School, where we had required chapel services twice a week. We always got to hear speakers from within our school or community. I can remember to this day some of the talks that stood out. Those were powerful moments in a young life.

Later on in life, I would attend the Wilmington sports writers' dinner—and I still carry with me vivid memories of some of the speakers.

As a student at Wake Forest University in Winston-Salem, North Carolina, the two most important courses I took were not in my major field. They were elective courses, with classes held up in the old theater district atop the library, under Professor James Walton. One course was An Introduction to Speech; the other was called Oral Interpretation of Literature. Those two courses impacted me so deeply that it carries on to this day. Professor Walton got us up on our feet, helped us fight through the fear (public speaking remains the number one fear in America) and helped us cut loose and express ourselves in front of our classmates.

In the early 1960s, when I first got into professional sports, I had the opportunity to meet baseball's Bill Veeck, legendary owner of the Cleveland Indians, St. Louis Browns, and Chicago White Sox. Bill believed the best way to sell your team is to go out and talk to every group within a one hundred mile radius about that team. I bought in to his advice and started doing that in every city to which my career took me—first in baseball and later in basketball. That foundation has allowed me to build a whole second career out on the corporate speaking trail. In a nutshell, here's what I've learned about public speaking—or what Lincoln might call effective oral communication:

1. You have to have a topic that you have mastered and that is part of your life.

2. Get your message organized, with points your audience can follow clearly and be able to write good notes.

3. Practice, practice, practice. Work on your delivery, the tone of your voice, your facial expressions. It's show business folks—practice! Practice in front of a mirror, have video taken, record your voice and study it. Recruit brave friends who'll listen now and then and give you confidential, unbiased feedback.

4. Passion and energy always carry the day. Your enthusiasm for your subject will infect your audience. If it's not there, it will really infect it—the wrong way!

5. Be a storyteller—just like Lincoln! We are hard-wired to retain stories, not power points—thank goodness! As author Jack Canfield once told me, "People's brains Velcro to stories."

6. Have your opening and closing nailed. Know exactly how you're going to launch the speech and how you're going to land the plane at the end. By the way, the audience judges you in the first twenty seconds of your talk and either buy in or tune out. You *must* start with a bang.

People ask me if I still get nervous before a talk. Here's what I tell them: I've discovered that if your stomach's not churning, if you're not on edge, you're probably not going to give a good talk. I've found that if my blood is not worked up, I'm probably going to struggle.

Some nervousness, some tension, is important to really do a great job. Whenever I am getting ready to speak at a major corporate event, I feel just like an athlete in the locker room before a big game.

I need to get alone with a hot cup of herbal tea; I need to mentally review exactly what I'm going to say; I do my stretching drills, my favorite breathing exercises, and I've even got a facial workout. I call it the Pumpkin/Raisin drill, and I recommend it—but not where anyone can see you. I make my face extend, like a big jack-o-lantern, and then I scrunch it all up tight, like a tiny little raisin. I do that five or six times: P-U-M-P-K-I-N, raisin; P-U-M-P-K-I-N, raisin; P-U-M-P-K-I-N, raisin. It's like putting your face muscles on a stationary bike—they really come alive. Then once I get the first story or first sentence out, my stomach calms down. But a good adrenaline rush is important before I speak. If I don't have that stirring inside of me, my talk will not be as exciting and passionate as it should be. If I don't feel those butterflies in my stomach, I'm concerned.

To me, there's nothing more rewarding than walking into a room of strangers, whether it's thirty or 300. You've got sixty minutes with them. Their attitude generally is, "Does this guy have anything to say that's important? Anything that will add value to my life?" And sixty minutes later for people to come up and thank you and let you know how much you've impacted them, how much they can take away and apply to their life—I'm not sure there's a greater feeling in the world.

Lincoln Lessons for Today
Wisdom to Apply Right Now

1. **Acquire a desire to become a master orator.** Think about the great American leaders—men like Lincoln, Franklin Delano Roosevelt, John F. Kennedy, and Martin Luther King, Jr. Their speeches and writings were almost pure poetry.

2. **Determine to master words and language**—even if it's just one language!

3. **Think carefully about the words you use on a daily basis.** Do they lift up and encourage, or are they likely to wound and leave scars?

4. **Build up your vocabulary and build up your spirit.** Let the words you let loose be words that make a lasting, uplifting, inspiring difference.

CHAPTER 20:

ON FINISHING WELL

....

Lincoln's Logs, by Gene Griessman

When I first took the oath of office, the slave states of the Deep South had already seceded and formed a confederacy. The nation teetered on the brink of Civil War. I pled for reconciliation, but as you know, I did not succeed in persuading my Southern friends from departing.

But when I took the oath of office again in 1865, the end was in sight. Here is the way one newspaper account described what happened: "An immense crowd had gathered in front of the Capitol building. As the President rose from his chair, a roar of applause shook the air, and at that very moment, the sun, which had been obscured all day, burst forth and flooded the spectacle with glory and with light."

It seemed like an omen of better things to come, an omen that the mist of war was about to be burned away.

That day, I pled for understanding, compassion, and forgiveness— and ended with these words:

> *With malice toward none, with charity for all, with firmness in the right, as God gives us to see the right, let us strive on to finish the work we are in; to bind up the nation's wounds; to care for him who shall have borne the battle, and for his widow, and his orphan—to do all which may achieve and cherish a just, and a lasting peace, among ourselves and with all nations.*

Eight weeks to the day after those words were spoken in Washington, they would be repeated, at my funeral in Springfield.

Every man is said to have his peculiar ambition. Whether it be true or not, I can say for one that I have no other so great as that of being truly esteemed of my fellow men, by rendering my self worth of their esteem.

− A . L I N C O L N

Let me tell you about the last day. It was a Friday. Good Friday. Four years to the day after Fort Sumter had fallen. Spring came early to Washington that year, and many lilacs were in full bloom.

It was perhaps the happiest day of my life. One of my cabinet members said he had never seen me so cheerful, so content. There was good reason to feel that way. On the previous Sunday, Palm Sunday, word had come that General Robert E. Lee had surrendered at Appomattox.

The war was virtually over, the Union was saved, and slavery was on the road to extinction.

That morning, I met with my cabinet, little knowing that it would be for the last time.

We talked about the strong feelings of revenge that were present in the North. One northern leader said he hoped that there would be a rebel leader swinging from every lamppost in Washington.

Not I. I told my cabinet members I hope there will be no persecution, no bloody work after the war is over. Let none expect me to participate in killing or hanging any of them. We must extinguish our resentments if we expect to live in harmony and union.

That afternoon I asked Mary to take a carriage ride with me—just the two of us—down by beautiful Rock Creek. We talked about the future.

We had a son with a learning disability: Tad. I told Mary I had promised Tad that we would eventually return to Illinois when my term of office expired. I'd buy him a mule and a pony and he would have a little garden all his own.

Washington had been hard on us. I had been happier when I dug potatoes at twenty-five cents a day than I had been as President. James Buchanan told me when I was sworn in: "If you're as happy on entering this house, as I am on leaving it, you're the happiest man in the land."

When I ran for Congress, my opponent was a preacher. One night I slipped into the back seat of the congregation hoping he wouldn't see me. He did. He pointed to me and said, "Lincoln, you're on the road to Hell."

I didn't know then that hell would be a white house in Washington.

Nor did I know that I was being stalked by a famous actor, who that morning had made a trip to Ford's Theatre to prepare for my arrival—and my departure.

The play had already begun when we arrived at the theatre. It was about 8:30 p.m. As we made our way to our seats, they halted the performance. The orchestra played "Hail to the Chief." They gave us a standing ovation.

We sat down to watch the play.

It was a comedy. I remember I laughed a lot. It felt good to laugh again—like the old days before the War. During the third act, Mary snuggled up against me: "What will people say if they see me hanging on to you like this?" she said.

"I reckon they won't say anything. And if they do, it won't matter."

I have an irrepressible desire to live till I can be assured
that the world is a little better for my having lived in it.

— A . L I N C O L N

Then came the final scene, played by the talented actor. In one hand he held a steel dagger, in the other a small pistol. The actor crouched behind his victim. The actor squeezed the trigger.

The bullet came crashing into my skull and lodged behind my right eye.

The actor jumped to the stage. The actor said his lines: "*Sic Semper Tyrannis.* Thus always to tyrants."

For a stunned moment, some people thought it was part of the play.

Perhaps it was. Didn't Shakespeare say, "All the world's a stage, And all the men and women merely players"?

Frankly, they've made more of me in death than they should have.

My Secretary of War, Mr. Stanton, said, "There lies the most perfect ruler of men the world has ever seen." That probably was the first public compliment he had ever paid me.

But don't laugh. The same thing will happen to you. People who spent their lives criticizing you will think of something nice to say over you, when they're sure you can't come back to benefit from the compliment.

Somebody asked me, "Lincoln, how do you want to be remembered?" I told him I wanted to be remembered as a common man, an ordinary man, who spent his life pulling up thistles, and planting a flower where I thought a flower would grow.

I would like to leave you with this thought: Always bear in mind that your own resolution to succeed is more important than any other one thing. More important than talent, wealth, or connections—your own resolution to succeed is more important than any other one thing.

I happen temporarily to occupy this big White House.
I am a living witness that any of your children may
look to come here as my child's father has.

— A . LINCOLN

Living Lincoln: On Finishing Well
By Pat Williams

I became a serious Lincoln student as an adult. I have stood where he spoke at Gettysburg; I've visited his home in Springfield, Illinois; stood at the platform of the train station from which he left for the White House, never to return; and walked in front of his burial site. I've visited the Cooper Union in New York City and stood on the same stage where Lincoln made his famous speech in his first appearance on the east coast, prior to the 1860 election. That was a powerful experience for me. Nothing captivates me more, though, than visiting Ford's Theatre, to see where he was assassinated, and then walking across the street to the little home where he was carried and died the next morning, April 15, 1865, at 7:22 A.M. I've been there a number of times and it never ceases to rivet me. A few years ago I even hired Michael Kauffman, a Lincoln expert, who drove me through Maryland and Virginia along the John Wilkes Booth escape route.

We can't seem to get enough of Lincoln—our thirst to know about him cannot be quenched. I plead guilty! I read just about every book that comes out on Lincoln, and attend every lecture that comes around. We long to walk in his footsteps and hear his voice.

Whenever I go to Chicago, I always jog to Lincoln Park and stand in front of his statue, where I look at him and reflect. He is woven into our American legacy and in so many ways he is part of who we are today. Our hearts seem to beat a little stronger when we hear his name.

There is much we will never know about Abraham Lincoln's last days, but one thing is most certain—on the day he and Mary made ready to attend Ford's Theatre neither of them had an inkling it would be Abraham's last. Much has been written about his prescience and premonitions of early death, but he could not have known that on that April night in 1865—April 14, to be exact—that John Wilkes Booth would be waiting with an assassin's fanatical mission twisting in his heart.

Prior to that fateful day, as we've read, Lincoln expressed a strong desire to leave something of consequence behind, something that would make a lasting difference in this world—and he found that legacy in his desire to see the abominable practice of slavery ended, once and for all. To that end he stood strong in the face of fierce opposition, ridicule, and even the threat of a nation split in two—so strongly did he believe in his life's mission.

Less than a hundred years earlier, William Wilberforce had argued the slave's cause in the halls of England's Parliament—and argued and argued and argued. At times it must have seemed he would never be heard and that his cause would die with him. But Wilberforce recognized the need to fight for the right of all people to live free, and in time he successfully convinced Parliament to sign the Slave Trade Act (1807).

Wilberforce died in 1833, when Abraham Lincoln was just twenty-four years old. They never met in person, but history has made them allies in the cause of liberty and justice for all.

How do you want to be remembered? It's a question worthy of some consideration. For all of us will be remembered for something, as Lincoln said, either because of or in spite of ourselves. Why not be remembered for something you did remarkably well? What could that something be? Is there a cause you can champion, a need you can meet, a passion you can pass on to others?

Did you know, by the way, that slavery is still stealing lives on planet Earth? I was personally astounded to discover that fact, assuming, as I imagine most of us have, that it had been wiped out all those years ago.

In early 2008, I had Kay Warren, wife of Pastor Rick Warren, on my radio show to discuss her eye-opening book *Dangerous Surrender* (Zondervan 2007). I was stunned to learn from her that this loathsome practice is far from defeated. There are many dark places in this world—even right here in America—where precious lives are still held captive by corrupted hearts every single day. Perhaps it's time for more of us to lead like Lincoln and fervently pursue the total, global abolition of slavery, once and for all.

However you choose to connect your today with tomorrow, I hope you'll consider well the life lessons of Abraham Lincoln as presented in this book. Few leaders have led as well or as effectively as he—but with him as our model all of us can emulate leadership, the Lincoln way.

Don't hesitate—put these principles to work immediately. There's a world out there that needs your leadership touch. You don't need anyone to tap you on the shoulder or suggest it to you.

When Vince Lombardi was coaching the Green Bay Packers to their five NFL championship in the 1960s, every Thursday morning he would begin practice by saying, "Who's going to lead today?" That's a good question for all of us! More importantly, who's going to lead tomorrow?

Will it be you? Or you? Or you? With America's greatest president—Abraham Lincoln—as your guide, you can't go wrong.

Lincoln Lessons for Today
Wisdom to Apply Right Now

1. **Remember Lincoln's last day.** Like all of us, Lincoln could not know exactly when his last minutes would be. But because of the way he lived his life he is remembered as perhaps our greatest President.

2. **Consider carefully how you want to be remembered,** the goal that burns in your heart to achieve—then find a way to go after it.

3. Always bear this truth in mind—**your resolution to succeed at your life's mission is more important than any other one thing.**

ABOUT THE AUTHORS:

GENE GRIESSMAN

....

Gene Griessman, PhD, is a popular speaker at conferences around the world, and has been performing his one-man play, "Lincoln Live," since 1990—including at such venues as Ford's Theatre, at the Georgia Dome before an audience of 25,000, and aboard the aircraft carrier USS Abraham Lincoln.

An author of books on Lincoln, leadership, and time management, Griessman has taught and spoken internationally at such institutions as The College of William and Mary, North Carolina State University, Auburn University, Tuskegee University, Georgia Tech, and has served as Fulbright Professor of Anthropology at the graduate university of Pakistan (Quaid-i-Azam University, Islamabad). He is also an award-winning TV host of the TBS program "Up Close," for which he conducted interviews with some of the most famous and successful people in the world. He is a lifelong student of people.

Griessman appears as Lincoln in the CD Lincoln's Wisdom, and narrates the audio books, 99 Ways to Get More Out of Every Day and Lessons from Legends, including interviews with people such as Hank Aaron, Julie Andrews, Ray Charles, and Ronald Reagan. He has taught and spoken internationally, from conferences to boardrooms to class-rooms. Griessman is also an actor and playwright, winner of the Benjamin Franklin Award for his writing and the Kay Herman Legacy Award for his speaking, and a member of the Television Academy of Arts and Sciences.

"Lincoln is America's best-loved, best-known high achiever—from log cabin to White House—and he used the same achievement secrets that other successful individuals I've interviewed used," Griessman explains.

PAT WILLIAMS

....

Pat Williams, L.H.D, is the senior vice president of the NBA's Orlando Magic and has spent over forty-six years in professional athletics. He's an in-demand motivational public speaker with an international audience, and is father to nineteen children. A marathon runner, devoted reader, and diehard baseball fan, he is also the author of more than fifty-five books that focus primarily on teamwork, leadership, parenting, and personal improvement. Pat has presented his leadership principles before audiences at many Fortune 500 companies, has been a featured speaker at two Billy Graham Crusades, and has spoken at two Peter Lowe Success Seminars.

A veteran of the U.S. Army, Pat helps teach an adult Sunday school class at First Baptist Church of Orlando and hosts three weekly radio broadcasts. He holds a B.S. from Wake Forest University, a M.S. degree from Indiana University, and a doctorate in humane letters from Flagler College in Florida. Pat and his wife, Ruth, live in Winter Park, Florida.

....

Peggy Matthews Rose has partnered with Pat Williams on the books *Read for your Life* (2007, Health Communications, Inc.) and *How to Be Like Walt*, written with Jim Denney (2004, Health Communications, Inc.). Her background includes many years writing and editing for Disneyland, The Walt Disney Company, and Saddleback Church, as well as for a variety of individual clients. Peggy also worked with Pat Williams and his daughter Karyn on the soon-to-be-released book, *The Take Away*, offering an intimate look at life lessons from a father to a daughter.

Additionally, Peggy has collaborated with a Saddleback Church pastor on two books about each person's unique purpose in life. A leader with an Orange County, California writers' community, she is a graduate of Cal State Fullerton and holds a BA in English Literature with a strong emphasis in journalism.

ACKNOWLEDGMENTS

With deep appreciation I acknowledge the support and guidance of the following people who helped make this book possible:

Special thanks to Alex Martins, Bob Vander Weide and Rich DeVos of the Orlando Magic.

I have been highly honored to collaborate with Dr. Gene Griessman on this book. He is a giant in the world of Mr. Lincoln, and it has been a joy to work with him.

Thanks also to our writing partner Peggy Matthews Rose for her superb contributions in shaping this manuscript.

Hats off to four dependable associates—my assistant Latria Leak, my trusted and valuable colleague Andrew Herdliska, my ace typist Fran Thomas, and my longtime adviser, Ken Hussar.

Hearty thanks also go to my friend Adam Witty and his fine team at Advantage Media Group. Thank you all for believing that we had something important to share and for providing the support and the forum to say it.

And finally, special thanks and appreciation go to my wonderful and supportive family. They are truly the backbone of my life.

— PAT WILLIAMS

When I first began performing Lincoln, I received and took some advice from Ralph Archbold, who already had become the definitive Benjamin Franklin. Archbold told me to strive to be more than an actor. Use an actor's tools and techniques, he said, but be a professional speaker—that is use the character of Lincoln to deliver a message that will help people.

His advice has made me different from many often talented, sincere, dedicated Lincoln impersonators, re-enactors, and Lincoln look-alikes. In a sense, I have turned Lincoln into an inspirational speaker, mentor, and coach.

I deeply appreciate those who gave me hours of their time helping create this book: Ken Futch, Austin McGonigle, and my daughter Sharon Griessman.

And finally, most of all, I acknowledge Pat and Peggy. Thank you, Pat, for seeing an opportunity, and making it happen, and you, Peggy, for taking the pieces of a puzzle and turning it into a picture that I am proud to have a place in.

— GENE GRIESSMAN

TreeNeutral™

Advantage Media Group is proud to be a part of the Tree Neutral™ program. Tree Neutral offsets the number of trees consumed in the production and printing of this book by taking proactive steps such as planting trees in direct proportion to the number of trees used to print books. To learn more about Tree Neutral, please visit **www.treeneutral.com**. To learn more about Advantage Media Group's commitment to being a responsible steward of the environment, please visit **www.advantagefamily.com/green**

Lincoln Speaks to Leaders is available in bulk quantities at special discounts for corporate, institutional, and educational purposes. To learn more about the special programs Advantage Media Group offers, please visit **www.KaizenUniversity.com** or call 1.866.775.1696.

Advantage Media Group is a leading publisher of business, motivation, and self-help authors. Do you have a manuscript or book idea that you would like to have considered for publication? Please visit **www.amgbook.com**